Awaken
Your Power
to Love

Awaken Your Power to Love

Richard A. Hunt
and
Joan A. Francis Hunt

THOMAS NELSON PUBLISHERS
Nashville • Atlanta • London • Vancouver

Published in Nashville, Tennessee, by Thomas Nelson, Inc., Publishers, and distributed in Canada by Word Communications, Ltd., Richmond, British Columbia.

The Bible version used in this publication is THE NEW KING JAMES VERSION. Copyright © 1979, 1980, 1982, Thomas Nelson, Inc., Publishers.

ISBN 0-8407-9260-3

Printed in the United States of America.

1 2 3 4 5 6 — 99 98 97 96 95 94

To our families
and
To couples everywhere

Contents

Acknowledgments

We are grateful for the support and encouragement of Lewis Smedes and Jarrell McCracken, whose vision and concern for couples and families opened the possibilities for this workbook.

We appreciate Victor Oliver, who has persistently believed in this project, advocated for it from the beginning, given many valuable editorial suggestions, encouraged us, and guided the project to its published form.

We especially recognize Brian Hampton, Lila Empson, and Marie Sennett for their support and help in expressing our ideas as well as their attention to the details that make this workbook more attractive and readable.

We thank the couples who were in the "Career, Marriage, and Faith" seminar in the Graduate School of Psychology of Fuller Theological Seminary for their encouraging suggestions and editorial reviews of the draft version of this workbook.

Introduction

Making Love Power Real for You

You have many good possibilities because God loves you and your spouse. God offers you power to grow in your love and life journey together. Love power is Christian love in action.

Using this workbook enables you to make these possibilities happen. Choose the parts that match the love power dimensions to your lives and marriage.

The table of contents gives you an overview of how love and power are expressed in every part of your marriage and your lives. Study this first so that you have a general understanding of the topics and possibilities available to you. Then begin your in-depth study with the section that is most important for you.

We recommend that you and your spouse work through this workbook together. You'll find lots of questions and fill-in-the-blank statements. For some of these you may want to use separate sheets of paper to record your answers. There are also charts and questionnaires; you may want to make a photocopy so that each person has a separate copy, or you may want to use a different color pen or your initials to keep each person's answers clear.

Begin by reading Part 1 for an overview of love power. Then go to the parts that are most interesting. Move back and forth to other sections that relate to you.

Choosing to love is choosing your future. From this faith perspective you select your resources and develop your skills to increase the positives in your marriage, which also eliminates negatives. This is the power for your love.

As you grow in your faith and skills, you can free your spouse to grow, also. In return your marriage becomes stronger because of your love freely given. As you become more competent and confident in your love power, you gain new perspectives and strengthen your marriage relationship.

These four major dimensions of love are connected through your communication skills. As you emphasize each dimension in your explorations, keep in mind that they are all interconnected in God's love.

Part 1

SHARING YOUR CARING

Using God's design for powerful love

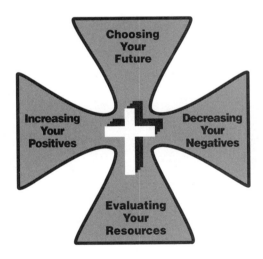

You are special as individuals and as a couple. There is no other couple quite like you. You become more special to each other in your life journeys together in marriage.

Love power produces these GEMS for couples:

G ifts for
E nriching your
M arriage:
S trategies and services for couples

P
L O V E
W
E
R

Creating a successful marriage is more a matter of being the right partner than of finding the right partner. The successful and joyous key is not, What can I get? but more important, What can I give?

2 SHARING YOUR CARING

Chapter 1

Love and Power

"So they married and lived happily ever after."

This is the usual storybook ending for couples. In many romantic stories and fairy tales we see the woman and the man becoming interested in each other, uncertain whether she will respond to his love or he will respond to her love. We may see the couple misunderstand and argue with each other, but sooner or later they usually make up just in time for the big wedding with all their friends wishing them happiness. Then they go off on their honeymoon. The story ends, but it is only the beginning.

What is your favorite romantic story? _____

Who are the woman and the man? _____

How did they meet? _____

What did they have to overcome to get married? _____

Who helped them? _____

Who tried to hurt them? _____

Why were they happy? _____

How did they achieve happiness? _____

What do you think happened to this couple? _____

Actually, your wedding is (or was) just the beginning of your life journey as a couple. You will probably live longer with your spouse than you did with your childhood family.

When many marriages end in divorce, and perhaps as many as half of the remaining marriages are troubled or unhappy, why does God continue to call us to a lifelong commitment to each other in marriage?

God gives us the power to love God and others as we love ourselves, as Jesus emphasized in the great commandments. Love God and love your neighbor as you love yourself.

This is love power. By God's loving grace, you and your spouse are neighbors who have the power to grow in love throughout your lives.

> P
> **L O V E**
> O
> W   *You shall love the LORD your God with all*
> E   *your heart, with all your soul, and with all*
> R   *your mind. . . . You shall love your neighbor*
>   *as yourself (Deut. 6:5; Lev. 19:18; Matt.*
>   *22:37–39).*

What is love? _____

Power and love are related by _____.

Your answer probably involves some type of family relationship. It may be a parent who cared for a child or a family member who fought in a war to protect our freedom and make the world safer for peace.

Your image of love may be the quick action of a brother or sister who saved your life, or the strength and warmth of a husband and wife who cared for each other across many years without counting the costs. The enduring support of a friend may also form your image of love.

We first learn about life, love, and power in our childhood families. From mother and father, we learn who we are, our language and customs, and what we can and cannot do. Only later do we realize that mother and father are spouses to each other, a couple. In a healthy family this marriage relationship is the foundation for parent-child and other family relationships. Through marriage, new families were formed as the children in your childhood families grew up.

Love and *power* are basic to success in your marriage.

Describe some ways you and your partner express love and power in your own special ways.

We express love by _____.

4 SHARING YOUR CARING

We express power by _____.

In this workbook you can check how well you are doing and discover ways to increase love even more across your life journey.

WHAT IS LOVE TO YOU?

Take a deeper personal look at love as you answer these questions.

What is the greatest experience of love that you have ever known?

_____

Which family relationships are
a special part of love for you? _____

How do they relate to your marriage now? _____

How do your family images blend with
your spiritual experiences (*for*
instance, God as a good Father or Parent)? _____

> **P**
> **L O V E**
> **O**
> **W**
> **E**
> **R**
>
> *Every couple is one of a kind, yet there are common basic elements that make the difference between success and failure in marriage.*

LOVE IN YOUR MARRIAGE

Think of one or two special love experiences that you have had with your partner. Separately describe one of these times, and then share your descriptions with each other.

When and where did it happen? _____

What was done? _____

What made it special? _____

How do you feel about it now? _____

How can you do it again? _____

What Do *You* Mean by Love?

Love has many meanings. In the following list, circle the words and phrases that best describe love for you. Mark an X through those that don't fit for you. Each person can use a different color pen to keep track of answers. Then talk together about your choices.

An alternate choice is to make a set of love word cards. Put one word on each card. Take turns drawing cards and making sentences expressing love using that word to each other.

Care	Concern	Sacrifice	Sensitive
Warmth	Dependable	Excited	Affection
Independent	Forgiving	Obey	Surprises
Cooperation	Hugs and kisses	Choice	Accepting
Attitude	Remembering	Keeping promises	Changeless
Sharing	Putting others first	_____	_____

P
L O V E
W
E
R

Greater love has no one than this, than to lay down one's life for his friends (John 15:13).

WHAT IS POWER TO YOU?

Think of a time when you very much wanted to accomplish a goal and did it.

Describe the situation: _____.

Some sources of power that I used to
reach that goal were _____.

6 SHARING YOUR CARING

When I think of power, it reminds me of _____.

Power is the ability and energy to express love. You may have both positive and negative reactions to power and strength.

My reactions to power are _____.

Other words for power are _____.

Power in Your Marriage

Review your description of your special love experience to see where power appeared.

Energy for love for me is _____.

I use energy to do good things like _____.

I have these skills for love: _____.

Resources that help me to love include _____.

Some Definitions of Power

Power may have many definitions and variations. In the following list, circle the words and phrases that best define power for you. Draw a line through the definitions that don't fit. Each partner can use a different color pen to keep track of answers. Then talk together about your choices.

Strength	Control	Possibilities	Sensitive
Resources	Energy	Schedules	Options
Skills	Abilities	Learning	Money
Manipulation	Personality	Appearance	Sex
Destruction	Improvements	Building up	Force

God has given you the power to love, the ability to do good for others as for yourself. You choose to love, and you select the resources to make love happen.

Love's direction to action for me is _____.

A goal I want to accomplish is _____.

I have this ability to implement goals with love: _____.

The power in *love power* is power to do, not power over someone. Love power is the ability plus the desire to cooperate together to cause good things to happen for both spouses in the marriage and for others the spouses influence.

> **P**
> **L O V E**
> **W**
> **E**
> **R**
>
> *Compared to being single, being married is like the difference between driving a car and reading about driving. Guided practice brings love power.*

SPECTATOR OR PLAYER?
YOUR M A P FOR YOUR MARRIAGE

Would you rather watch a championship game or play on your own team? As a spectator, you gain knowledge and insights about how champions play the game. As a player in the action, you try out the ideas and make them your own. On the basis of feedback from your practice, you decide to throw out some of the insights, keep other ideas, and improve them.

Growing your love and power in your marriage is being a player after having observed others in their marriages. There are three key elements in your marriage MAP—models, attitudes, and practice.

Models: Knowledge and Understanding. You have observed many couples, beginning with your parents. Out of these observations you have formed models or images of what a healthy couple is like. Observe how they do their marriage, and learn the concepts they use. Identify the steps that create the patterns you see.

Persons who are models for our marriage are _____.

Attitudes: Aware of Your Feelings. You also have attitudes about these models, both positive and negative. Notice how you feel about the results you observe.

Which results do you like or dislike? _____

Practice Actively. Once you decide which models you like, you can practice the good patterns and eliminate the bad patterns in your marriage. Plan ways to learn skills and to get the resources you need. Practice a new change, get feedback about it, and shape it to accomplish your goals.

A pattern I will practice in our marriage: _____.

A pattern I will avoid in our marriage: _____.

P
L O V E   *When things go right, we know what we*
W   *can do next time. And we increase our*
E   *power to love.*
R

To make good skills your own, information is not enough. It helps to have a coach who can give accurate feedback about how you are doing when you practice. You and your partner can agree to practice and to give each other feedback about the results. You can coach each other.

Sources of Your Marriage Models

Consider some sources of your marriage models and attitudes. Then decide whether and how you will practice them for yourself.

	Pattern	*Attitude (Like/Dislike)*
Parents	_____	_____
Relatives	_____	_____
Friends	_____	_____
Movies, TV	_____	_____

Persons who are available when I need them include _____.

I need to see another way out of (*for instance, my problem*) _____.

This affects the ways I give or receive love by _____.

Each spouse has the power to build or destroy the relationship, the power to choose to love or to hate the other.

Think about some couples you know who are happy and successful in their marriages. Contrast these couples with other couples you know who are unhappy and dissatisfied with their relationships.

What do you think makes the difference? _____

This workbook can help you and your spouse read your life and marriage MAPs. As you clarify how love and power are expressed in your models, attitudes, and practices, you can choose goals and ways to reach them that will bring you satisfaction and happiness.

On a journey there are always many ways to get from where you are to where you want to go. In your marriage journey, there is always more than one way to do something. It is important to agree on your goals and then free each other to do them. Having choices and freedom to implement them builds confidence and trust.

> **P**
> **L O V E**
> **O**
> **W**
> **E**
> **R**
>
> *Through our choices, we can reduce the power of the past and commit ourselves to growing in love and becoming the persons God calls us to be.*

Strong love freely given builds marriage bridges. When you value and encourage each other, your marriage grows.

In your marriage many steps will enable you and your spouse to reach the goals you want.

What step (or steps) will you take to reach your goal? _____

Chapter 2

Your Journey as a Couple

"Marry me and we will sail through life together," said he.

"And where are we going?" she inquired.

"Wherever you want to go," he affirmed.

"Is that where you want to go, also?" she asked.

"It doesn't matter where, so long as you are there," he crooned.

"Then how will we know when we have arrived if we don't know where we are going?" her head asked. "That doesn't feel good," her heart added.

As a couple, you and your spouse are on a life journey together. Where are you going in your marriage? In your life? Is your spouse going the same way or a different route? Maybe you are not going anywhere.

Where I think our marriage is going: _____.

Where my spouse thinks our marriage is going: _____.

I am directing my life toward _____.

I think my spouse's life is directed toward _____.

P **L O V E** **W** **E** **R**	*I take you as my spouse, from this day forward, for better and for worse, for richer and for poorer, in sickness and in health, to love and to cherish, till we are parted by death.*

Where do you mark the beginning of your life journey as a couple? How important for you, and for your spouse, is each of these markers?

Event	Effect on Me	Effect on My Spouse
Wedding	_____	_____
Engagement	_____	_____
Other events:		
_____	_____	_____
_____	_____	_____
_____	_____	_____
First date	_____	_____
Earlier markers:		
_____	_____	_____
_____	_____	_____
_____	_____	_____

STAGES OF YOUR JOURNEY

There are several interrelated ways to look at your marriage across your life span. You can focus on your ages, the ages of your children, your career stages, and/or your involvement in leisure activities. Each perspective can help you put your marriage in broader contexts and cope with the changes that occur.

How do you feel about your age? _____

How does your spouse feel about your age? _____

How do you feel about your spouse's age? _____

Another way of tracking your adult journey in marriage is with the significant events of your lives. Compare your time line to the typical steps or stages in marriage that are noted on the next page.

12 SHARING YOUR CARING

	Big Events for Wife	*Big Events for Husband*
Twenties *(for example, choosing a life work, preparing for career, choosing a mate, having children)*	_____ _____ _____ _____	_____ _____ _____ _____
Thirties *(for example, career changes, children in school, deepening roots)*	_____ _____ _____ _____	_____ _____ _____ _____
Forties *(for example, children in college, children leaving home, parents' illnesses, "life half over")*	_____ _____ _____ _____	_____ _____ _____ _____
Fifties *(for example, grandchildren, health problems, potential retirement, new career, travel)*	_____ _____ _____ _____	_____ _____ _____ _____
Sixties and older *(for example, deaths in family, integrating life, reengagements)*	_____ _____ _____ _____	_____ _____ _____ _____

Which changes do (or did) you welcome? _____

Which changes do (or did) you dread or dislike? _____

Which changes do you wish you could change? _____

Which events occur (or occurred) earlier or later than usual? _____

How do you feel about these changes? _____

YOUR JOURNEY AS A COUPLE 13

If you look at your marriage according to your children's ages, you may mark the stages of your marriage in these ways.

Children's Ages	How Wife Feels About This	How Husband Feels About This
Before children	_____	_____
Infants, preschool	_____	_____
Elementary ages	_____	_____
Middle school ages	_____	_____
High school ages	_____	_____
Late teens, early twenties	_____	_____
"Empty nest"	_____	_____

CHANGES: STABLE TIMES AND TRANSITIONS

You may mark the changes of your marriage journey in terms of how you feel about each other and your marriage. As you can explore in more depth in Part 2, these markers probably relate to your commitment to each other and to God as you grow in the knowledge and understanding of the life journey to which God continues to call you.

A marriage or life stage consists of a stable time in which spouses know what to expect next and are satisfied with their patterns and habits. The stage boundary occurs with some type of transition in which the old patterns no longer work and one or both spouses search for better ways to love and more power to reach desired goals.

You can see this basic life dynamic in your marriage as a series of relatively stable times marked by crises and changes to which you must adjust. These changes may be brought by your personal growth, by attainment of a goal (such as completion of career preparation or a move to a different city), by births, deaths, or divorces among members of your extended family, or by other important life changes.

Each change or crisis offers you the opportunity to integrate new elements into your marriage. Choosing not to grow in love and power leads to disintegration of your lives together.

By choosing to grow as you journey together, you can find additional reasons to grow together in love and create more skills for making your marriage successful and happy.

Where we now are in our marriage journey: _____.

Some transitions we have already faced and worked through: _____.

A challenge we now face (or will soon face): _____.

How I want to respond to that challenge: _____.

Your marriage journey is through uncharted seas. In this sense it is a classic, heroic journey in which you find renewed power to face and overcome hateful dragons and other adversaries to win the joys and peace of deeper love for your spouse, yourself, and others in your life. Your quest always involves leaving the familiar (hence "family") world, facing unexpected challenges, reaching into the depths of your soul to find insights, strength, and determination, and bringing renewed and deepened love to those around you.

P	
L O V E	*Do not deprive one another except with consent for a time, that you may give yourselves to fasting and prayer; and come together again so that Satan does not tempt you (1 Cor. 7:5).*
W	
E	
R	

THREE STEPS TO MARRIAGE MASTERY

Along your journey, you will become more skillful as you increase your power to love each other. New or unexpected challenges motivate you to learn more about marriage.

As you talk with other couples, you find that many of them are doing well in their marriages without much help, and some couples can be guides to help other couples. Some couples, however, are still trying to learn the basics, with or without much help from others.

Nearly every couple fits each of these levels of marriage skill according to which area of the relationship is considered. These three levels of marriage are similar to the centuries-old method of learning a trade, profession, or skill. Many unions still use these terms:

1. The *apprentice* is learning a trade or skill under the guidance of other, more skilled workers.

2. The *journeyman* or *journeywoman* has achieved a level of experienced, reliable, and competent work with little supervision needed.

3. The *master* has achieved a high level of competence and knows the skill well enough to be qualified to teach others.

Master:
Couples who can teach love power to other couples.

Journeyman:
Couples who regularly practice and grow in their love power skills.

Apprentice:
Couples who decide to learn and improve their basic skills for marriage.

A time in our marriage when I feel
most like an apprentice or beginner is _____.

A time in our marriage when I practice
the art of marriage like a journeyman is _____.

A time in our marriage when I know enough
to mentor or teach another couple about marriage is _____.

QUALITIES OF SUCCESSFUL COUPLES

Think about the most satisfied couples you know. What are the qualities that make these couples stand out as being especially successful in their marriages?

Consider the following list of possible characteristics of successful couples. Add others to the list. Then on each row, circle one number to show the factor's importance for success in marriage.

Importance for Success in Marriage

	None	Little	Some	Much	Very Much
Reach desired goals	1	2	3	4	5
Do things together	1	2	3	4	5
Disagree rarely	1	2	3	4	5
Be involved in community	1	2	3	4	5
Have children	1	2	3	4	5
Have a good job or career	1	2	3	4	5
Resolve conflicts well	1	2	3	4	5
Maintain a mutually satisfying sex life	1	2	3	4	5
Manage finances well	1	2	3	4	5
Agree on goals	1	2	3	4	5
Be committed to each other	1	2	3	4	5
Joke and laugh together	1	2	3	4	5
_____	1	2	3	4	5
_____	1	2	3	4	5

How do you and your spouse blend these characteristics into your marriage?

_____

_____

SUCCESSFULLY MARRIED COUPLES HAVE DIFFERENCES

You and your spouse may not always agree, and you may have had some difficult and troublesome times, but if you are still together, and still glad you are together, you have an important story to share with other couples.

Some of our imperfections: _____.

Some of our better qualities: _____.

A successful marriage validates a couple's wisdom about marriage and the hopes for others.

HOW ARE YOU DOING IN YOUR MARRIAGE?

Marriage checkups provide preventive maintenance, just as health or automotive checkups prevent major problems later. Use the following list of marriage skills to examine how you and your spouse see your marriage now.

Answer each question individually. Then after both wife and husband have answered, compare answers.

On a scale of 1 (needs more work) to 7 (doing well), rate how well you are now doing in your relationship. Add other topics that are important to you, and rate them on the same scale. Use these letters to identify your rating on each item.

M = Man rating himself   H = Woman rating man
F = Woman rating herself   W = Man rating woman

	Needs More Work					*Doing Well*	
How I Think We Are Doing in This Area:							
Reaching goals we choose	1	2	3	4	5	6	7
Increasing the good we want	1	2	3	4	5	6	7
Stopping the bad we don't want	1	2	3	4	5	6	7
Using our resources well	1	2	3	4	5	6	7
Work and career issues	1	2	3	4	5	6	7
Daily lifestyle patterns	1	2	3	4	5	6	7
Children and parenting	1	2	3	4	5	6	7
Communication	1	2	3	4	5	6	7
Conflict resolution	1	2	3	4	5	6	7

	Needs More Work					Doing Well	
Affection, support, care	1	2	3	4	5	6	7
Financial management	1	2	3	4	5	6	7
Leisure activities	1	2	3	4	5	6	7
Relatives and friends	1	2	3	4	5	6	7
Religious involvement	1	2	3	4	5	6	7
Spouse cooperation	1	2	3	4	5	6	7
Sexual relationship	1	2	3	4	5	6	7
_____	1	2	3	4	5	6	7
_____	1	2	3	4	5	6	7

To benefit from your checkup, first celebrate with your partner the areas where you agree in positive ways on your ratings. Then consider areas where your ratings differed, and thank each other for the courage to express differences. Then create a plan to continue the positives, and use them to replace any negatives.

We celebrate these positives: _____.

We have these differences: _____.

Here are ways we can use our positives
to change our negatives: _____.

COURAGE FOR YOUR JOURNEY

Have you ever felt like giving up and walking out of your marriage? Yes ___ No ___
If so, you are both honest and normal. Times of discouragement are a normal part of every marriage. How you handle discouragement can give you encouragement to continue your marital journey.

I felt like leaving my marriage when _____.

I did/did not leave because _____.

A friend who helped me in that situation was _____.

Some ways my church or other groups
encouraged me and/or my spouse were _____.

YOUR JOURNEY AS A COUPLE 19

You can renew your courage and increase your love power for your marriage journey. It is encouraging to know that couples can have the joy of making up after a big argument. It is encouraging to see couples overcome difficulties and crises. You can discover how they cope with the ups and downs of their marriages by observing them and talking with them.

Among your friendship networks, you need at least four other couples as friends and models for marriage. From these couples, you find their sources of courage.

> **P**
> **L O V E**
> **O**
> **W**   *Wait on the Lord; be of good courage, and*
> **E**   *the Lord shall strengthen your heart*
> **R**   *(based on Ps. 27:14).*

FOUR IMPORTANT COMPARISONS FOR YOUR MARRIAGE

You can gain perspective on what is now happening in your marriage by looking at couples who are at different ages and stages in their marriages. You can learn from them as well as discover that they probably have just as many discouragements and encouragements as you have.

You can benefit from couples in each of the following four categories. Take a few minutes to write their names and notes about what they have given to you. If possible, find a way to thank them for the gifts of insight and encouragement that have been meaningful to you.

1. Similar Age

With couples your own age, you can share activities, exchange child care, and compare notes about your stage in life and marriage. Think of a couple about your same age and in similar circumstances.

Name of this couple: _____.

Ways these partners usually handle frustrations in their marriage:

_____.

Something they do well that I would like to modify to use in our marriage:

_____.

2. Next Stage

Now think of a couple a few years older than you.

Name of this couple: _____.

Ways they usually handle frustrations in their marriage:

_____.

Something they do well that I would like to modify to use in our marriage:

_____.

In this couple you may be able to see what might be coming to you just around the next age and stage bend. Observing couples who are about five to ten years older than you enables you to preview possible next stages in your marriage, parenting, and career.

If you have younger children, you can see how your friends parent their children who are starting to school, struggling through puberty, learning to drive, and leaving home for college or marriage.

3. Previous Generation

Think of a couple about the same age as your parents (but not your parents).

Name of this couple: _____.

Ways they usually cope with frustrations in their marriage:

_____.

Something they do well that I would like to modify to use in our marriage:

_____.

It is very freeing to see which family patterns were peculiar to your parents and which patterns are typical of the previous generation. This couple can also share stories proving that the romance and upsets that seem so new to your generation existed in their parents' and grandparents' generations as well. It helps to realize that earlier generations overcame difficulties, played pranks, and enjoyed life, and that they lived through them.

4. Much Younger

You can also learn from a couple younger than you are. They may have used their resources or opportunities in creative ways that inspire you to cope better with your own situation.

Name of this couple: _____.

Ways these partners usually handle frustrations in their marriage:

_____.

Something they do well that I would like to modify to use in our marriage:

_____.

You need to know real-life couples whose lives say to you, "You *can* do it! It is worth the work to grow and learn how to deepen your love for each other. We are still learning this, and we want to encourage you to do it."

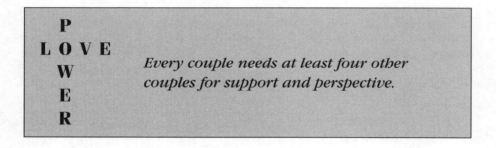

P
L O V E
W
E
R

Every couple needs at least four other couples for support and perspective.

DIRECTION OF YOUR JOURNEY

Along your life journey, you are often faced with choosing which fork in the road to take. If you have an accurate map of where each fork will lead, you can make better choices. You can get this information from others who have made similar choices. They can describe to you how they felt about their choices, the goals they chose, and the resources they used or needed.

Some persons who have given, or can give, information to me about consequences of their choices are _____.

Which goals did they choose? _____

What resources did they use or need? _____

What were the results? _____

How does that relate to you? _____

Chapter 3

Emotions and Marriage Satisfaction

"I'm so dissatisfied with my marriage," Jan groaned to her friend, Valerie.

"I know what you mean," replied Valerie. "I also have a model husband."

"You're so fortunate," Jan exclaimed, looking a bit puzzled.

"Sorry, but you missed my comment," replied Valerie. "A model husband is a small imitation of the real thing."

Happy. Successful. Satisfied. These words and their opposites often are used to describe marriage. Like Valerie, some may rate their marriages as small imitations of success and happiness. How do you rate your marriage?

Our marriage is _____.

When you say you "have a good marriage" or you "wish things were better," you are comparing what is happening to what you want to happen. *Satisfaction* is when the *actual* (reality) matches (or exceeds in the desired direction) what you *expected* or wanted. When you evaluate a marriage, you have made a comparison between what you see and what you expected to see. Your criteria for a successful marriage are the yardsticks you use to measure how well you are doing.

When I say "good," I mean _____.

A "good marriage" includes _____.

Love and power are the criteria for a successful, happy, healthy, and satisfying marriage. In a good marriage, both spouses continue to experience love and power as the two major dimensions of marriage.

HOPE FOR YOUR MARRIAGE

As you were growing up, you formed dreams and expectations about what your marriage would be like, long before you met your spouse. Your spouse was also creating dreams and images of an ideal marriage. As you searched for the spouse of your dreams, your dream person was also searching for you. Maybe you are trying to be that "dream spouse" now.

> **P**
> **L O V E**
> **W**
> **E**
> **R**
>
> *We accept tribulations, knowing that tribulation produces perseverance; and perseverance, character; and character, hope. Now hope does not disappoint, because the love of God has been poured out in our hearts by the Holy Spirit who was given to us (based on Rom. 5:3-5).*

Dreams give hope. When you see some of your dreams come true and know how you helped them to happen, you increase your confidence and hope that you can reach other dreams.

Hope is very powerful because it pulls your mind, body, and spirit together toward a common life-renewing goal.

I experienced the power of hope when _____.

DREAMS DESCRIBE YOUR MARRIAGE STANDARDS

Dreams are a dramatic way of describing where you want to go or perhaps other directions to avoid (as in nightmares!). Dreams, hopes, aspirations, and expectations are your anticipations about the future, your criteria for successful marriage.

Dreams and goals are basic to your marriage relationship and your lives together. You began to form your life dreams in childhood and continued to shape them through your teenage years. Your spouse was in the same process long before you met and married.

My important dream is _____.

My spouse's important dream is _____.

These dreams have changed in several ways: _____.

I have these feelings about these dreams: _____.

As individuals and as a couple, you choose your life directions. Throughout adulthood, you will continue to reevaluate and modify your hopes and dreams as you compare them with your accomplishments and disappointments at later stages in your lives.

As you will see in more detail in Parts 2 and 4, your dreams are related to how you see yourself in relation to your family background and your heritage. Out of these experiences you also have developed your faith relationship with God. In a sense, your dreams are your faith for the future, just as your family and ethnic heritage is your faith from the past.

> **P**
> **L O V E**
> **W**
> **E**
> **R**
>
> *A wife is not to depart from her husband. But even if she does depart, let her remain unmarried or be reconciled to her husband. And a husband is not to divorce his wife (1 Cor. 7:10–11).*

Fairy tales seldom describe what the couple expected to happen or what actually happened. These stories assume we all want to be happily married and know how to do it.

Expectations are the standard by which you judge whether your marriage is satisfying, happy, and successful.

I feel too many expectations concerning _____.

Who sets my standards? _____

Some standards I hold strongly are _____.

Reality (the actual) is what you perceive as happening. You construct your own reality out of your interpretation of events. Reality for you is not necessarily the same reality your partner sees, but both of you may be right about the essentials of what you see.

For instance, if you expect your spouse to give you at least three hugs every day, and your spouse really does give you more than three hugs per day, you will rate your marriage as happy or good. If your spouse does not give you any hugs, you will rate your marriage as unhappy or unsatisfying.

Something I expect from my marriage: _____.

How much I get this: _____.

EXPECTATIONS AND HIDDEN AGENDAS

When you compare what you get with what you wanted, you judge how satisfied, happy, and successful you are. Your judgments involve both thinking and feeling elements.

Expectations are the details of your marriage covenant or contract. You have at least three levels of expectations, assumptions, and predictions about your marriage.

1. *Conscious and expressed expectations* are the topics, plans, hopes, and dreams that you and your spouse discuss openly with each other. These are your shared images of marriage.

An expectation I have shared with my spouse is _____.

2. *Conscious but unexpressed expectations* are ones that each partner has but keeps secret from the other. Every spouse has some expectations and hopes that are not yet expressed to the partner. You may have both healthy and unhealthy reasons for not talking about them. Maybe you are afraid of what might happen, you may not want to hurt your partner, or you may consider the topic unimportant.

You probably have some expectations you are not yet ready to share with your partner. This is normal and natural in every marriage. However, there may be something you are ready to share now.

An expectation I will share with my spouse soon is _____.

How I feel about expectations I
have not yet shared with my spouse: _____.

3. *Partially aware, hidden, and unknown expectations* are ones that neither you nor your partner can see well. These unconscious contracts become the

hidden agendas of marriage. Every person has them. You get clues to them when you feel dissatisfied, disappointed, or let down but cannot state reasons for your emotional reaction.

P
L O V E
O
W   *Good communication means that the*
E   *impact on the listener matches what the*
R   *speaker intended.*

A feeling I sometimes have that
I would like to understand better is _____.

WANTS AND GIFTS

Wants and gifts are another way you can identify the expectations by which you judge the success of your marriage.

Wants arise out of your goals and out of your unfulfilled desires from earlier in your life. A want may not be the same as a need.

Wanting a cookie is different from needing a cookie, but wanting some kind of food may be the same as needing nourishment. This provides a wonderful opportunity to rationalize wants into needs. For example, needing a new car when the one you have is in very good shape is more likely a matter of wanting a new car.

Something I want from my spouse is _____.

Something I really *need* from my spouse is _____.

Gifts are the resources and talents that overflow from who you are. Gifts are the ways you use your power to nourish and care for your spouse. Gifts are also your potentials for problem solving.

What I want to give to my spouse is _____.

What I will give my spouse is _____.

How you perceive your gift may be different from how your spouse receives it and evaluates it according to personal hopes and dreams. The gap between what you intended and its impact on your spouse is the key to knowing whether your gift satisfies your spouse.

Think of a recent situation that was satisfying for you and/or your spouse.

Situation: _____.

In this situation, what I
intended to give to my spouse was _____.

What I think my partner wanted from me was _____.

The impact of my gift on my partner was _____.

In this situation, what my spouse experienced from me was _____.

Compared to my spouse's want or need, my gift was _____.

This analysis can help you to be aware of how your behavior affects your partner. It is looking at what you do from your spouse's viewpoint. You can use a similar analysis of what your spouse gave to you.

> **P**
> **L O V E**
> **W**
> **E**
> **R**
>
> *If you then, being imperfect, know how to give good gifts to your spouse and children, how much more will your Father who is in heaven give good things to those who ask (based on Matt. 7:11).*

Think of a different situation that was satisfying for you and/or your partner.

Situation: _____.

What my spouse intended to give to me was _____.

What I wanted from my partner was _____.

As compared to my want, my spouse's gift was _____.

What I actually experienced from my partner was _____.

My comparison of my spouse's intended
gift with my experience of it was _____.

This second comparison can help you appreciate the intentions of your partner, especially in situations when your spouse meant well even though you did not like what happened. "It's the thought that counts" is true. In addition, learning how to give makes the thought even more genuine.

SATISFACTION, EXPECTATIONS, AND EMOTIONS

Your emotions are based on your past experiences as you remember them. Your emotional logic is never exactly the same as your partner's logic because each has different experiences. Where the past experiences were similar, both probably have similar emotional reactions to the same current situation.

Name an emotion that is important for you: _____.

Describe two or three situations when
you are most likely to have this emotion: _____.

Before sharing these situations, invite your
spouse to consider the same emotion: _____.

Ask your spouse to describe situations
when this emotion is experienced: _____.

Then compare notes to see similarities and differences.

Your basic emotional dimension is good vs. bad or satisfied vs. dissatisfied or positive vs. negative. God created you with a capacity to design and modify your personal standard for what is good or bad. For this reason, Jesus said, "Love your neighbor as yourself" (Matt. 22:38). The golden rule also expresses this guide for living as treating others, including your spouse (who is also your neighbor in Christ), as you would like them to treat you (Matt. 7:12; Luke 6:31).

> P
> L O V E   *Just as you want others to do to you, you*
> W   *also do to them likewise (based on Luke*
> E   *6:31).*
> R

You grow in love by expanding your definition of love and by increasing your skills for caring about others. In your personal spiritual growth you can examine your images of love. These are your expectations or standards for caring and nourishing yourself, your spouse, and others.

If you know how to love yourself in the context of God's love, you will have some idea of how to love others since their need for love is probably as great as is yours. God knows that if we apply the same standard to others as we use for ourselves, we will have a fairly good guide to love power. This is a *fairly good* guide because your standards have been heavily influenced by your past experiences, which need to be reevaluated again and again.

Consider a situation in your marriage, and then answer these love power questions about it:

In what ways is it good or bad? _____

How can you control it to
increase the good and reduce the bad? _____

Positive emotions are joy and hope. When you want love and have the power to get love, you experience joy, fulfillment, and satisfaction.

You experience hope when you don't want something bad to happen, such as hate or rejection, and yet have the power to prevent the bad from happening.

Negative emotions are rage and fear. When you don't want something and can't avoid getting it (such as pain), you experience rage.

You experience fear when you want love and acceptance but do not have the resources to get them.

> **P**
> **L O V E**
> **W**
> **E**
> **R**
>
> *There is no fear in love; but perfect love casts out fear, because fear involves torment. But he who fears has not been made perfect in love (1 John 4:18).*

How do you want to modify
these statements to fit your views? _____

Love is the value that guides your future. Love is the standard for judging which actions are positive and worth repeating again. On the basis of genuine love you also identify patterns that are negative and need to be reduced or eliminated.

A way to picture this is with the Joy-Hope-Fear-Rage box. Describe an example of each of these four possible combinations.

When you experience joy you are able to continue a desired situation.

An example is _____.

When you experience hope, you are able to change an undesired situation.

An example is _____.

When you experience fear, you are not able to keep a desired situation.

An example is _____.

When you experience rage, you are not able to stop an unwanted situation.

An example is _____.

JOY *comes from being able* to continue something that you want to keep. This gives openness, esteem, and confidence.	HOPE *comes from being able* to change something that you do not want. This gives cooperation, vision, and determination.
FEAR *comes from being unable* to keep something that you want to have. This brings withdrawal, escape, and paralysis.	RAGE *comes from being unable* to stop something that you do not want. This brings depression, panic, and destruction.

YOUR EMOTIONAL THERMOSTAT

You control the temperature of your home by adjusting how much heat or coolness your heater or fan produces. You may do this automatically with a thermostat. You set the temperature you want, and the thermostat then adjusts the furnace or air conditioner to that temperature.

In some ways your emotions are your personal thermostat for your marriage. You have some ideas about what you want and what you will give, and you attempt to live to make those results happen.

Think of a fun or joyful situation with your spouse. Then identify how it expresses love, esteem, or acceptance, and identify what each of you does to make this happen.

A joyful or fun situation is _____ .

The ways it expresses love or acceptance are _____ .

Now think of a situation in which you felt fear or rage with your spouse; then identify how it consists of a lack of love and/or power.

A fearful or rage-filled situation is _____ .

The ways it expresses lack of love or power are _____ .

FROM EVALUATION TO ACTION

On the basis of your evaluation of the situation, you decide to take action. Your emotions magnify your views and motivate you to move in some way.

If the situation is pleasant, joyful, and fun, you probably will move toward or with your spouse. You can stay close or move closer because you know it is safe and comfortable. And by moving closer, your spouse sees you as safe and positive.

If the situation is unpleasant or hurtful, calling forth your fear, anger, or rage, you will probably move away from your spouse. If you cannot get away, or if you think you can get away with it, you then may turn and attack your spouse.

If your spouse counterattacks, sooner or later one of you will get away from the other's threatening harm. This escalates into a downward spiral, an increasingly hurtful and dangerous pattern that you must stop if you want your marriage to stay alive and healthy.

A downward spiral we sometimes have is _____ .

It affects these persons: _____.

Some ways I would like to change this are _____.

As emotion, love mobilizes you to embrace and join your spouse. It increases your hope for more good situations. Later when you remember these good times, you will know how to make them happen again. This is love power in action.

How love gets me into action: _____.

As emotion, anger mobilizes you to attack and separate from the source of your fear or anxiety. Later when you remember these dangerous times, you will know what you did to escape and will avoid getting that close again.

How anger gets me into action: _____.

Action is your power to affect your spouse in loving and caring ways that nurture your spouse to greater confidence, maturity, sensitivity, and intimacy with you.

Positive nurture releases the energy and resources you formerly used in fear and anger responses so you can use that energy in loving responses that generate hope.

When you expect good results and things happen as you wanted, you feel satisfied and pleased, and your self-esteem continues high because you are in control.	When you expect poor results but things happen much better than you expected, you feel puzzled and surprised, yet your self-esteem may go down because of undeserved success.
When you expect good results but things do not happen as you wanted, you feel dissatisfied and angry, and your self-esteem goes down.	When you expect poor results and things happen as you expected, you feel depressed and trapped, and self-esteem continues low.

<table>
<tr><td>

P
L O V E
O
W
E
R

</td><td>

Satisfaction is closing the gap between your expectations and your experience (reality).

</td></tr>
</table>

BREAKING THROUGH ANGER TO LOVE POWER

Out of your commitment to your spouse, you can choose to replace anger with a solution.

Consider a situation when you became angry: _____.

1. *Discover the real reason you are angry.* This is the function that anger has for you, given the way that you see yourself, your spouse, and the situation.

In that situation I was angry because _____.

The danger that situation had for me was _____.

My anger protected me by _____.

2. *Find the places where you are feeling attacked by your spouse.*

When I am feeling angry with my spouse, I see myself as being attacked in these ways: _____.

It reminds me of other times and/or other persons who attacked or hurt me: _____.

3. *Find the places where your spouse is feeling attacked by you.* If you are feeling attacked, your spouse is probably feeling attacked by you.

If you actually intend to attack or hurt your spouse, clarify what motivates you to do this. If you are not trying to hurt your spouse, consider how you can change your words and actions to reach your goals and still make the process safe for you and your spouse.

My spouse may be seeing me as the attacker in these ways: _____.

My goal in the situation was _____.

I can make these changes in my words
that make it safer for my spouse and me: _____.

I can make these changes in my actions that
make it safer for my spouse and me: _____.

4. *Give this three-part breakthrough response.* The breakthrough response begins with your reaffirmation of your love for your spouse, followed by your feelings and wants in the anger-producing situation, followed by your second reaffirmation of your love. Some call this the *sandwich approach* in which you surround difficult messages with twice as many affirmation and support messages. Of course, the positive loving messages must be genuine and honest.

a) I do love you in these ways: _____.
(As you say this, turn to your spouse, smile, and clasp hands.)

b) Right now when _____.
(Clearly describe the situation, behaviors, and your interpretations of them.)

I am feeling _____.
(Give feedback about your feelings, such as feeling attacked, pushed, put down, hurt, ignored, misunderstood.)

And I want _____.
(Describe your intentions, such as to affirm and support your spouse, to let your spouse know you hear the views, or to take a break so both can return to solve this situation soon.)

And the topic or issue I want to talk about is _____.

c) And I really do love you because _____.
(Add warmth, touch, good humor, and appreciation for your spouse.)

After you express this with your spouse, be open to reversing roles.

Chapter 4

The Four Love Power Dimensions

"You really don't know what it's like to live," commented John as he and Paul were walking to their next tee.

Reaching for his best driver, John continued, "I've known many women, played the field, and married three times. You're still stuck in your first marriage. Look at what you're missing!"

"Look at what I'm missing!" exclaimed Paul, his mouth dropped in disbelief at John's comment. "Ann and I have been married sixteen years, we have three wonderful kids, and we are having a ball. Sure, we have our rough times, but I wouldn't trade places with you in a million years. Look at what you're missing!"

Are you more like Paul or John? _____

What factors would lead each
man to make the statements he did? _____

What might Ann or the
women John has known say? _____

How would you like to change their
statements to fit your experience? _____

Using and studying this workbook can greatly improve your chances for a happy and satisfying marriage. You and your spouse decide whether you will succeed in your marriage. You shape where you will be next week, next month, and in the years ahead through the ways that you connect these four basic dimensions in your relationship.

THE FOUR LOVE POWER DIMENSIONS

The four love power factors are choosing your future, increasing your positives, evaluating your resources, and decreasing your negatives. Through your communication, you connect these to create your successful marriage. All of the major topics and issues in marriage appear in these love power dimensions.

Love emphasizes creating your future in the ways you live today. *Love* is the overall goal or purpose. Learning to love is the ultimate purpose in life (for example, 1 Cor. 13; Rom. 12). God gives us marriage as a major laboratory for learning to love.

Power is the means to the goal of love, the way to cause love to happen. It is having the abilities and resources to produce loving actions. Under God, you use your power to implement your faith and live the life to which God calls you.

Try your hand at describing what makes the difference between couples who create successful, fun-filled marriages that last across their lives and couples who destroy their relationship and divorce.

Happily married couples
have these qualities: _____.

Unsuccessful couples who
divorce have these qualities: _____.

ORGANIZING LOVE AND POWER FOR ACTION

God has given you the ability to organize your life along the major love power dimensions of values and resources. Your values are the end goals you seek. To say that you want a loving, enjoyable marriage means you value these good results. You express these values in your goals.

My values and goals express love in these ways: _____.

Power is the strength that comes from your resources for reaching the goals you want. When you act in love, you are applying your skills and resources to show care and support to others. This is the powerful love that we call love power.

I use my resources to implement love in these ways: _____.

A BRIEF CHECKUP FOR YOUR MARRIAGE

You can see where you are now on these major love power dimensions. Take a moment to note ones in which you are doing well and where you need help. To identify your answers, use different colors. As an alternative, one of you can circle your answers and the other can draw a square around the answer.

There are five clusters of questions. These correspond to the four love power dimensions that communication connects. Relate your results to the chapters you choose to emphasize.

W = Wife H = Husband	Need Much Help	Need Some Help	Doing Fairly Well	Doing Very Well	Could Help Others	Have Helped Others
Choosing Our Future						
Building a solid foundation for our marriage	1	2	3	4	5	6
Personal faith, choosing standards for living the life given to me	1	2	3	4	5	6
Our commitment as a couple, living our vows as life partners	1	2	3	4	5	6
Helping the next generation, from our kids to children everywhere	1	2	3	4	5	6
Reaching out to others in our neighborhood, community, and world	1	2	3	4	5	6
Careers, both paid and unpaid, and how we implement the future	1	2	3	4	5	6
Total marks in each column	____	____	____	____	____	____
Increasing Our Positives						
Multiplying our good times	1	2	3	4	5	6
Affection and sex, intimacy, touch, physical affirmations of each other	1	2	3	4	5	6
Money and finances, both getting income and budgeting expenses	1	2	3	4	5	6
Basic lifestyle patterns and habits, residence, schedule, daily activities	1	2	3	4	5	6

W = Wife H = Husband	Need Much Help	Need Some Help	Doing Fairly Well	Doing Very Well	Could Help Others	Have Helped Others
Leisure and fun times, relatives, friends, well-being, recreation	1	2	3	4	5	6
Making good out of bad, coping well with crises and things we don't want	1	2	3	4	5	6
Total marks in each column	___	___	___	___	___	___

Evaluating Our Resources

	Need Much Help	Need Some Help	Doing Fairly Well	Doing Very Well	Could Help Others	Have Helped Others
Managing our abilities and strengths	1	2	3	4	5	6
Genetic traits: physical appearance, disabilities, chronic health concerns	1	2	3	4	5	6
Personality patterns: expectations, habits, roles, rules, social skills	1	2	3	4	5	6
Families of origin: our parents, siblings, and/or other relatives	1	2	3	4	5	6
Ethnic, racial, national, and/or cultural factors or concerns	1	2	3	4	5	6
Support networks: our involvement in community, church, school groups	1	2	3	4	5	6
Total marks in each column	___	___	___	___	___	___

Decreasing Our Negatives

	Need Much Help	Need Some Help	Doing Fairly Well	Doing Very Well	Could Help Others	Have Helped Others
Replacing hurtful patterns with healthy skills	1	2	3	4	5	6
Abuse and addiction issues: alcohol, other drugs, food abuse, gambling	1	2	3	4	5	6
Violence in our home: physical, sexual, verbal, neglect	1	2	3	4	5	6

W = Wife H = Husband	Need Much Help	Need Some Help	Doing Fairly Well	Doing Very Well	Could Help Others	Have Helped Others
Extramarital sexual affairs, sex addictions, pornography	1	2	3	4	5	6
Depression and other mental health conditions, emotions, losses, deaths	1	2	3	4	5	6
Losing our marriage through withdrawal, neglect, or divorce	1	2	3	4	5	6
Total marks in each column	___	___	___	___	___	___

Connecting the Four Dimensions

	Need Much Help	Need Some Help	Doing Fairly Well	Doing Very Well	Could Help Others	Have Helped Others
Increasing our skills for communicating love	1	2	3	4	5	6
Speaking for ourselves, clearly expressing emotions, wants, actions	1	2	3	4	5	6
"I" and "you" messages, being aware of effects of my actions on others	1	2	3	4	5	6
Acting on clear and positive values and standards	1	2	3	4	5	6
Good problem-solving skills, able to resolve conflict well	1	2	3	4	5	6
Able to share viewpoints and opinions comfortably	1	2	3	4	5	6
Total marks in each column	___	___	___	___	___	___

You can score your answers in two ways:

1. For each dimension, enter the total number of answers you and your partner marked in each column. Each column total can be from 0 to 12. The higher the column total, the more you emphasize that rating.

2. Calculate the overall agreement score for each dimension by first finding the difference between your and your spouse's answers to each statement. For ex-

ample, if on a particular statement you answered 2 and your spouse answered 5, the difference is 3 (ignore the negative sign). Then add up the six numbers. For each six statements your total agreement score can range from 0 to 30. A low score means your ratings generally agree, and a high score suggests that you and your partner do not see your marriage in the same ways.

Share your feelings about your scores, and then describe what led you to rate each item as you did. Use these results to guide you to the chapters you consider more important for you to explore first.

YOUR SUCCESS SPREADS TO OTHER COUPLES

You may discover that other couples are looking to you and your spouse to find hope, insights, and encouragement. These other couples may be your relatives, friends, work associates, or neighbors who are struggling to make their marriages succeed and are looking to you for help.

Regardless of whether you want to be an example to another couple, you probably already are. As your children observe how you and your partner are doing your marriage, they are forming patterns they will take into their future relationships. As others talk with you, they may be searching for clues about marriage to guide them.

As you become more successful in your marriage, your success can spill over to others who want to know how you do it.

CELEBRATE!

We hope you have decided that you want to celebrate your happiness and make changes in your relationship that will be even more satisfying along your lifetime marriage journey.

The appendix describes how you can obtain additional computer and video multimedia games and aids for exploring topics in this book.

Some thoughts and feelings
about our marriage journey: _____.

What I think being a whole person means: _____.

What my spouse thinks being a whole person means: _____.

How these views relate to our marriage: _____.

Part 2:

CHOOSING YOUR FUTURE

Building a solid foundation for your marriage

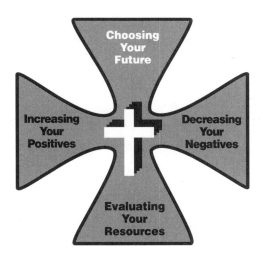

CHOICE IS CENTRAL

Choices shape your future. God gives you the power to choose which meanings you give to life events and how you will respond to them. God has also set limits on your choices, such as placing you on this planet at this time.

What are your feelings about your choices? You may feel pleased, scared, optimistic, or angry about some decisions you want to make or must make. Often you have to make choices before you know what the results will be.

How I feel about making choices: _____.

Areas where I want more options: _____.

Areas where I have too many choices: _____.

To make better choices, I need _____.

Choices have three aspects: goals, resources, and results. You choose goals, and you select the resources you need to reach the goals. The real or potential results of the resources you apply to your goals influence your choices.

Goals give options among specific future possibilities. Goals set the context for your choices. For example, if you want to be a teacher, you must have a teaching certificate, which usually can be obtained only by completing a college degree. Given that career goal, your choices are where to go to college, which classes to take, and how you will complete your education.

What are three important goals you have right now? _____

What decisions do you need to make to reach each goal? _____

Resources are the talents, skills, and habits you have developed in your past experiences. Having more experience and skills gives you many more options and increases your power to choose.

Describe three or four talents, abilities, or skills you now have:_____.

What other resources do you have, such
as health, money, and/or credit? _____

What other factors affect your resources,
such as the economy, timing, or opportunities? _____

Results occur as a combination of the resources you bring to reach the goals you choose in your situation. When results are good, you may see them as rewards or gains. When results are bad or unpleasant, you probably see them as punishments or losses.

Choosing your future means that you know that you have at least two or three real alternatives ahead of you, each with its own set of consequences.

Results I would most like to have: _____.

Losses I most want to avoid: _____.

Chapter 5

Personal Faith

Looking at her husband, Charlie, Jenny smiled. "Your eyebrows are tense, and you seem like you are far away in space. A penny for your thoughts."

"I feel trapped in so many ways," groaned Charlie.

"Such as?" Jenny continued.

"Well, whether to switch jobs or get more training. Just what do I want to be when, or if, I ever grow up?" Charlie slowly began.

"Sounds familiar. I feel that way at times, also," she added. "Yet it is nice to know that we have choices."

"Yeah, but some choices are so difficult. If only I could see what would happen by making a specific choice," Charlie replied.

"Well, some are easy. I choose you for sure," said Jenny as she reached her hand into his. "And I know God wants us to learn how to make good choices, and I am with you."

"That helps a lot. Thanks. I love you, too," Charlie softly affirmed. "So, how will we decide about some of these choices? Are you ready for a leap of faith?"

Because your choices determine your future goals and whether you reach them, your personal faith is the foundation of your marriage.

You express your faith through the goals you choose. Your faith is your assumptions about life and where marriage fits into human existence. Every person has some type of faith system.

Your faith system is the basic element of your marriage. It is the "I" in the "I statements" that you make, the trust you place in the universe, the basis of existence on which you build your foundation for living. Your words are not your faith but the pointers to your faith.

Your faith is your inner core, gut-level convictions about yourself, your spouse, and others in relation to God, the Creator, Redeemer, and Sustainer of the universe.

Faith is expressed in your relationships with others, with the world, and with God.

I express my faith in these ways: _____.

The direction I choose for my life is _____.

I will be more likely to control the results I get by _____.

> **P**
> **L O V E**
> **O**
> **W**
> **E**
> **R**
>
> *Your faith system is the place where you stand to view the world and to move the world.*

SOME SYNONYMS FOR FAITH

Circle two or three of the following meanings of faith. Then talk with your partner about how they help you describe your personal feelings and attitude about faith.

- Belief involves cognitive, intellectual assent, such as "I believe" means "I live by"; I think or consider that to be "true" or real; or I assert or agree that something or someone exists.
- Hope transcends expectations and is enveloped by a promise deeper than words ("faith, hope, love" [1 Cor. 13:13]).
- Trust is crossing a bridge built by knowledge in a leap of faith.
- Mystery is an encounter with new dimensions of life.
- Action means doing something or making a commitment.
- Promise implies a vow, pledge, troth, guarantee, and/or bond.
- Obedience carries with it the idea of "oughtness" or of being compelled.
- "Wholth" means wholeness, health, and worth, and it embodies confidence as the opposite of anxiety.

FAITH FACTORS

Your faith is the key to your marriage. From a faith perspective, each partner decides whether to make the marriage succeed or fail.

Ways my faith guides our marriage: _____.

Ways my spouse's faith guides our marriage: _____.

STYLES OF FAITH

What kind of faith do you have? Your faith system begins at birth. Research shows that three basic personal styles give rise to corresponding styles of faith.

1. Secure/Hopeful

If others usually reached out to you and freely gave you warmth, comfort, and nurture, you developed basic trust and hope about yourself and life. You feel secure and optimistic about your future.

Times I am secure and hopeful in my faith: _____.

Ways I can share this security
and hope with my spouse and others: _____.

2. Avoidant/Fearful

If others were cold or hurtful and caused you pain, you tried to avoid them (and others who seemed like them) because you feared being hurt again. You develop mistrust, become pessimistic about the future, and avoid commitments.

Times I avoid others and am fearful of them: _____.

Ways I try to nurture my spouse
and others so they will not avoid me: _____.

3. Anxious/Uncertain

If others were sometimes nurturing and sometimes harsh and hurtful, you became anxious and ambivalent about them because you never knew whether the next encounter would bring pleasure or pain. You have anxiety and uncertainty about the future, which lead you to be unpredictable and to change your commitments to fit the moment.

Times I feel anxious and uncertain about others: _____.

Ways I try to support my spouse and others
so they will feel less anxious and fearful: _____.

Regardless of the roots of your faith, you can nurture your personal faith and your partner's faith, so you can both grow in your love and power.

The many experiences and encounters of childhood and adolescence increasingly confirmed you in one of these three basic styles, with a secondary influence from one of the other styles. Most of the time you are in one faith position, yet occasionally you drift into one of the others until the next event reconfirms you in the approach that seems to explain most of your experiences.

My primary faith position is _____.

I also find myself in the position of _____.

A major way in which you express your faith is through religion. Religion refers to (1) your personal faith, (2) your involvement in a religious group, and (3) your commitments in your daily life.

PERSONAL DIMENSIONS OF FAITH

Credo is an ancient word that means "I believe." Every person has a credo, a personal faith statement. You may express your beliefs in your own words, or your credo may be set in historic words, such as the early Christian affirmations. To say "I believe in God the Creator, Redeemer, Sustainer" or "God the Father, Son, and Holy Spirit" clarifies who you are in your marriage and who your partner is.

To affirm that nothing can separate us from God's love (Rom. 8:38–39) implies that both you and your partner are loved by God and are neighbors to each other. To seek to love God and love your neighbor (Lev. 19:18; Matt. 19:19; Gal. 5:14) means you want to love your spouse, who is also your neighbor.

Choosing your future begins with your personal faith. Scripture often uses "the heart" to refer to one's personal faith, assumptions, soul or spirit, and basic views about life. For example, "out of the heart proceed evil thoughts, murders, adulteries, . . . false witness, blasphemies" (Matt. 15:19). Out of the heart are all the issues of life.

Out of your faith come your values, your respect for persons, property, environment, and all the world around you.

Ways I respect and value persons are _____.

Ways I respect and value property are _____.

Ways I respect and value the environment are _____.

Ways I help to bring peace and safety are _____.

We choose to love because we have first been loved by others. God wants to give love to others through you, just as God gives love to you through others. In this is the power of love, the love power for your marriage and your journey through life. This is your faith decision, which is the basis for your lives together in marriage.

Defining Faith for Myself

Here are some statements about faith. Mark each statement to show your views about faith. Invite your spouse to answer independently. Then talk together about your personal faith and how it relates to your marriage and to the world about you.

	Agree	Maybe	Disagree
Faith involves value judgments, such as negative or positive, desirable or undesirable.	_____	_____	_____
Faith asks, "Good for whom?" Good for me, for us, for all, hurtful to no one.	_____	_____	_____
Faith is a relationship with God.	_____	_____	_____
Faith is personal—each "I" is born, one person at a time; each "I" dies, one at a time.	_____	_____	_____
Faith can never be proven, only lived.	_____	_____	_____
Faith changes and grows and matures throughout one's life.	_____	_____	_____
Faith is relative, just as big is to small, happy is to sad.	_____	_____	_____
What satisfied us at age 2 or 12 may not satisfy us at age 22, 42, or 72.	_____	_____	_____
Personal faith guides the type of person you decide to be for your partner in marriage.	_____	_____	_____

> **POWER**
>
> *Let us love one another, for love is of God, and everyone who loves is born of God and knows God. . . . There is no fear in love, but perfect love casts out fear. We love because God first loved us (based on 1 John 4:7, 18–19).*

RELIGIOUS GROUP DIMENSIONS OF FAITH

A religious group is formed by persons who have common or compatible views about faith, God, worship, values, traditions, and actions. When you and your spouse participate together in a church, you find support for your marriage and encouragement in times of difficulty. You can also offer inspiration to others through your church activities. And exploring your faith at home strengthens your relationship.

Ways in which we celebrate our faith with others at church or in another religious group:

Church groups in which my spouse and I participate: _____.

Worship services (weekly, monthly, yearly): _____.

Church leadership roles: _____.

Teaching children, youth, or adult classes: _____.

Other ways: _____.

Ways in which we celebrate our faith at home:

Daily devotional: _____.

Prayer at mealtimes: _____.

Personal or family prayers: _____.

Talk about values and other faith issues: _____.

Other ways we are concerned about spiritual involvement: _____.

Ways our marriage expresses our faith: _____.

COMMITMENTS IN YOUR DAILY LIFE

Commitment means that you decide to do something and then work to make it happen. Commitment is your will and determination to hold to important values and ideals.

You make personal commitments in each of these three areas of religion. You blend these unique dimensions of spiritual growth together when you make commitments to each other and to others.

I reach upward to God when _____.

I reach inward to myself when _____.

I reach outward to others when _____.

In these ways you continue to move through the many stages of faith that are part of your growing and maturing faith.

P
L O V E
W
E
R

I believe in God who is Creator of the universe and all that is, Redeemer of the world and all persons everywhere, Sustainer, Comforter, and Guide to those who will follow. In God we live and move and have our lives.

Chapter 6

Commitment as a Couple

"When I make a commitment, I intend to stick with it," affirmed Bill.

"No matter what happens?" Bette asked. "Does that include our marriage?"

Bill gently put his arms around Bette and drew her closer. "It most certainly includes us. I love you a lot now, and I want to love you even more every year for the rest of our lives."

"Ditto," said Bette. "That really means a lot to me. I love you always, and I will never leave you."

"Really?" Bill questioned, half in jest. "I like the safety and security of your presence and promise."

Your commitment to your spouse is a major way you express your faith. What you think and feel about marriage vows in general greatly affects your specific commitment to your spouse.

On the basis of your faith, you form your assumptions about marriage.

For most Christians, marriage is based on a strong love power faith. In Mark 10:1–12, Jesus states God's intention that a man and a woman be joined in marriage from which there is no divorce. However, since men and women sometimes are unwilling to learn to love each other, divorce is a concession to their "hardness of heart," or refusal to be open to growth and renewal in the relationship.

Christian support for unconditional commitment to lifelong marriage with no divorce is not merely a legal matter or a concern about sex, children, or the hurtful results of divorce. Rather, lifelong marriage with no exits enables both partners to maximize love.

NO EXIT IS YOUR MARRIAGE GUARANTEE

Your wedding is your official public announcement and confirmation that you really are serious about your marriage. You make public your commitment to God and your mutual commitment to each other. Persons present are more than just witnesses to your pledges. They represent the support of relatives and friends who, knowingly or not, make their vow to support and encourage you as a married couple.

Your wedding also signifies God's blessing to you, which bonds you together as two growing persons who form a corporate unit or body. Through your marriage, God ties you together so that you can be free to grow in your love for each other.

Having families and friends
present at our wedding means _____.

Searching for a loophole or escape from marriage is the hardness of heart that Jesus described.

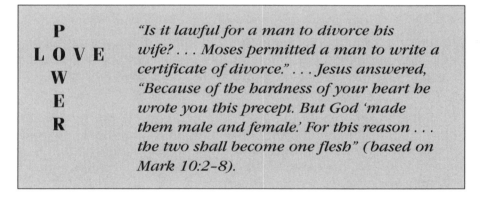

P
L O V E
W
E
R

"Is it lawful for a man to divorce his wife? . . . Moses permitted a man to write a certificate of divorce." . . . Jesus answered, "Because of the hardness of your heart he wrote you this precept. But God 'made them male and female.' For this reason . . . the two shall become one flesh" (based on Mark 10:2-8).

God also knows that there will be times in every marriage when both husband and wife will want to escape from the marriage rather than do the difficult work of learning new love power solutions.

The foundation reason for "no divorce" is to encourage both spouses to learn to love and grow in their power to care and share. Like a wise and loving parent who pushes a child to good experiences even when the child does not want to grow up, God lovingly encourages you to discover and create love in your marriage.

How I feel about "no exit" from marriage: _____.

To grow in marriage, both spouses must close all exits and block the escape routes. A basic purpose of marriage is to learn to empower love in both yourself and your spouse. This is the fundamental reason for no divorce. Such a challenge takes much work over many years.

Your vow of faith says that you will learn to love your spouse, you will keep trying, you will be sensitive to the impact of your actions on your spouse, and you will keep searching for ways to let your spouse know of your love.

This "no exit" view of marriage probably seems tough and difficult unless you have experienced it yourself. You may have already experienced such unconditional love at times from your spouse and from others.

A specific way in which my partner has been there or been present for me at a time that I especially valued and appreciated: _____.

Some ways that I have been there and supported my spouse, even when it was hard for me to do so: _____.

Marriage is one way we choose to experience and learn the power to love. Most wedding services include a vow or promise similar to this:

> I (*Name*) take you (*Name*) to be my (*husband/wife*), from this day forward, for better or worse, richer or poorer, in sickness or health, to love and to cherish, and forsaking all others, till we are parted by death, and thereto I give you my solemn vow.

In this vow each partner is saying, "I completely commit myself to you. I pledge to you my entire self (my troth or trust or fidelity), all that I am and have, without reservation. I will stay with you. I will close off all exits that I might use to escape from this commitment. I promise to be your spouse, and nothing this side of death will prevent me from keeping this promise to you."

It is quite a big promise, yet it frees you and your spouse to be open, honest, vulnerable, and caring for each other. It opens far more possibilities than it closes.

For me, wedding vows mean _____.

Two spouses form a two-person corporate body (or corporation) called marriage. This is the "one flesh" or "one unified body" consisting of the two very real individual spouses. Although part of a corporate body, each spouse continues to be a distinctive person who chooses to learn to live with the other in love.

Betrothal comes from *troth,* which means "total commitment, loyalty, pledged faithfulness, and solemn vow." By exchanging this vow, each spouse is both giving and receiving a trust, which often is signified in giving and receiving rings or other symbols.

MY ASSUMPTIONS ABOUT MARRIAGE

Here are some statements that are often made about marriage. Add others to the list. Then on each row, circle one number to show how much you agree or disagree with it.

Marriage is . . .	Strongly Disagree	Dis-agree	Neutral	Agree	Strongly Agree
A laboratory for love.	1	2	3	4	5
An opportunity to grow.	1	2	3	4	5
A way to guarantee sex.	1	2	3	4	5
A union to produce children.	1	2	3	4	5
A trap for spouses.	1	2	3	4	5
Beyond our control.	1	2	3	4	5
Full of conflicts.	1	2	3	4	5
A romantic challenge.	1	2	3	4	5
Controlled by finances.	1	2	3	4	5
A happy challenge.	1	2	3	4	5
A refuge from the world.	1	2	3	4	5
_____	1	2	3	4	5
_____	1	2	3	4	5

Some of my other assumptions about marriage: _____.

Some of my spouse's assumptions about marriage: _____.

MAKING YOUR MARRIAGE PROMISES REAL

Promises point to possibilities for change. What are some specific promises you can make to your spouse that you can actually do? Some may be on a weekly basis.

In the next week I will _____.

In the next year I will _____.

On a more regular basis I will _____.

Consider all of the implications of choosing a spouse. That person comes with a variety of perspectives, hopes, fears, expectations, wants, and dreams. Consider these possibilities as they apply to your spouse.

My spouse's hopes: _____.

My spouse's fears: _____.

My spouse's dreams and interests: _____.

My spouse's habits and skills: _____.

My spouse's relatives I value: _____.

Some important influences (such as
hometown, school, friends): _____.

How my spouse feels about . . .

     money: _____.

     sex: _____.

     politics: _____.

     career: _____.

     leisure: _____.

     other: _____.

Consider the same possibilities as they apply to you. (You'll need to write answers on a separate sheet.)

Marriage gives you the opportunity to explore these similarities and differences on which you continue to decide your future.

SUPPORTS FOR YOUR COMMITMENT

You have at least three major supports for making your commitment happen. These are personal standards ("who I am"), relationship satisfaction ("what is hap-

P **L O V E** **W** **E** **R**	*The one changeless aspect of life and of marriage is change. Marriage changes every day, week, month, and year. These changes are marked by birthdays, disagreements, sexual fireworks, placid evenings, rest and recreation, nourishment, and renewal.*

pening between my spouse and me"), and opinions of others ("what others think or say about me or us").

1. "Who I am" is the inner, personal set of standards. These are your decisions or standards regardless of the circumstances. Write some examples of personal standards. (*For example, divorce is out of the question for me, or when I give my word, I stick with it.*)

No matter what happens, I will _____.

Regardless of the results, I will not _____.

2. "What is happening between my spouse and me" concerns what occurs in your marriage, the results of your interaction with your partner. (*For example, we try to do what's best for both of us.*)

I am very satisfied with _____.

The thing I most like about being with my spouse is _____.

3. "What others think or say about me or us" refers to what you think others want you to do or not do in your marriage, and what they want to happen to and for you both. (*For instance, my family wants me to stay with my partner, or my mother or father or friends think my marriage will work out.*)

Which relative or friend has a
strong opinion about your marriage? _____

Concerning my marriage, this relative or friend thinks _____.

Even though relatives, friends, or other outside forces may want something, the more important concern is how you will cope with those pressures. By building your marriage on a no-divorce, no-exit foundation, you pledge yourselves to grow in love power as you cope constructively with outside forces that seek to separate you.

How I feel about forces that
might harm our marriage: _____.

How I feel about forces that
seek to help us in our marriage: _____.

Commitment is your motivation to accomplish specific goals. This motivation may come from within a person or outside a person. When commitment is externally imposed, a person probably looks for escapes and exits from that commitment. When commitment comes from within, you feel as if you have freely decided to stay with your partner.

How I feel about my promises to my partner: _____.

A specific change in my commitment: _____.

DIMENSIONS OF COMMITMENT

Since commitment and vows are so important for your marriage, the following questionnaire may help you clarify sources of your commitment. Circle the number that most closely matches your response. (Each spouse may want to use a different color.)

	Agree	Maybe	Disagree
1. My family wants me to leave my spouse.	1	2	3
2. In the future I may want to change partners.	1	2	3
3. It is difficult for me to talk with my spouse.	1	2	3
4. My relationship with my spouse comes before anything else.	1	2	3
5. Divorce is out of the question for me.	1	2	3
6. If my spouse knew certain things about me, it might destroy our relationship.	1	2	3
7. My partner and I have many good plans for our future.	1	2	3
8. Others want me to stay with my spouse.	1	2	3

	Agree	Maybe	Disagree
9. When I give my word, I stick with it.	1	2	3
10. I am more attracted to others than to my partner.	1	2	3
11. I prefer to keep my options open rather than stay with the same spouse throughout life.	1	2	3
12. In our relationship, we try to do what's best for both of us.	1	2	3

P
L O V E
W
E
R

Commitment is your opportunity to grow.

Key for Dimensions of Commitment

Use the answers you marked to find your commitment levels.

The higher the number on your "us" scale, the more you and your spouse make mutual decisions and stand together. A low score suggests that you and your spouse need to grow in your mutual decision-making skills.

Add answers for statements 9 and 12	=	_____
Add answers for statements 1 and 6, then subtract from 8	=	_____
This is your "us" scale score.	Total:	_____

The higher the number on your "others" scale, the more other people support you and your spouse in your lives and marriage. A low score suggests that you and your spouse need to enlarge your network of positive support from others for your marriage.

Add answers for statements 4 and 7   = _____

Add answers for statements 2 and 10, then subtract from 8   = _____
This is your "others" scale score.   Total: _____

The higher the number on your "inner" scale, the more dependable and pre-dictable you are in making promises and commitments. A low score suggests that you need to strengthen your inner resolve and determination to keep your vows.

Add answers for statements 5 and 8   = _____
Add answers for statements 3 and 11, then subtract from 8   = _____
This is your "inner" scale score.   Total: _____

For each scale, your score can be between 4 and 12.

> **P**
> **L O V E**
> **W**
> **E**
> **R**
>
> *The fruit of the Spirit is love, joy, peace, longsuffering, kindness, goodness, faithfulness, gentleness, self-control. Against such there is no law (Gal. 5:22–23).*

SOME SPIRITUAL LIFE DISCUSSION STARTERS

Faith and marriage are related in many ways. The following statements describe ways that spiritual and religious faith may be involved in your marriage. You and your spouse can answer these and then discuss your answers.

To identify each person's answers, you may make a copy of the page, or each spouse may use a different color pen to mark answers.

	Agree	Maybe	Disagree
In our marriage my spouse and I should . . .			
Pray together every day.	_____	_____	_____
Study the Bible together regularly.	_____	_____	_____
Discuss spiritual issues.	_____	_____	_____
Go to the same church together.	_____	_____	_____
Lead in family devotions.	_____	_____	_____

	Agree	Maybe	Disagree
Agree on theology.	_____	_____	_____
Pay tithe (10% of income).	_____	_____	_____
Attend church at least once a week.	_____	_____	_____
Pray for each other.	_____	_____	_____
Work together as a couple.	_____	_____	_____
Help others.	_____	_____	_____
Talk honestly about weakness.	_____	_____	_____
Encourage each other's spiritual growth.	_____	_____	_____
Encourage our children to attend church.	_____	_____	_____
Be aware of God's calling to work.	_____	_____	_____
Witness to others about our faith.	_____	_____	_____

Chapter 7

The Next Generation

After choosing your faith perspective and your life partner, the third major choice about your future involves the ways you relate to the next generation. Whether you have biological children or none, you have many children.

Children are the future because _____.

Two things we all must do for all children are _____.

P
L O V E   *Jesus loves the little children, all the*
W   *children of the world.*
E
R

No child is ever the exclusive property of the parents. No child is ever just "my" child. Since every child represents the union of a man and a woman, every child belongs to at least two persons. Since the persons must live responsibly within their neighborhood, society, and world, every child is ultimately the responsibility of us all.

I most care about these children: _____.

I am most worried about these children: _____.

I am most concerned about these adolescents: _____.

HELPING THE NEXT GENERATION

Here are some ways that adults help the next generation. Add others of your own, and then mark each to show whether it is something you are doing or will do.

After your spouse answers, you can explore these as you choose anew the ways you will affect the next generation.

Ways I Want to Help the Next Generation . . .	Not for Me	Maybe	Definitely for Me
Have children of our own.	_____	_____	_____
Adopt children.	_____	_____	_____
Be a temporary foster parent.	_____	_____	_____
Be a stepparent to my spouse's children.	_____	_____	_____
Be a Big Brother or Sister to a child.	_____	_____	_____
Spend more time with children.	_____	_____	_____
Give money to homes and agencies that serve children and youths.	_____	_____	_____
Work in the PTA in our school.	_____	_____	_____
Be a volunteer leader in youth groups, such as Scouts, Camp Fire, sports, church, etc.	_____	_____	_____
Help connect grandparents and grandchildren.	_____	_____	_____
Work for better television for children and youths.	_____	_____	_____
Campaign against violence, guns, drugs, and other harmful influences on youths.	_____	_____	_____
Urge and support parent education classes in schools, churches, and agencies.	_____	_____	_____
For my vocation, be a teacher, counselor, or school administrator.	_____	_____	_____
Serve on a board for a school or agency for children or youths.	_____	_____	_____
Raise financial support for those who work with children and youths.	_____	_____	_____

THE NEXT GENERATION 63

Ways I Want to Help the Next Generation . . .	Not for Me	Maybe	Definitely for Me
Create jobs or hire graduates of schools.	_____	_____	_____
Other: _____	_____	_____	_____
Other: _____	_____	_____	_____

PARENTING SKILLS AND QUALITIES

Good parenting takes skill, energy, thoughtfulness, persistence, confidence, and many more qualities. No matter what you do, your children will be a lot like you. A one-sentence book on parenting: *Decide on the type of person you want your child to be, and then be that person.*

There is far more to good parenting than can be presented in this brief chapter. However, good parenting is based on respect for every child as a person of worth in the sight of God and in the sight of the child's family, friends, school, and neighborhood. These attitudes are formed in each individual's experiences as a child and adolescent.

Consider some of the ways you received respect, love, and affirmation when you were growing up.

Ways I received respect as a child: _____.

Ways I received respect as an adolescent: _____.

It helps parents to talk together and agree on the guidelines both have for raising their children. Here are some possible guidelines for parenting. Check whether you usually agree or disagree with each guideline. Then discuss them with your spouse.

Good parents should . . .	Agree	Maybe	Disagree
Always tell their children what to do.	_____	_____	_____
Set few limits and follow through on them.	_____	_____	_____
Involve children in decisions that affect them.	_____	_____	_____
Listen to children's fears, worries, and wants.	_____	_____	_____
Let the children settle their own arguments.	_____	_____	_____
Compliment their children when they do well.	_____	_____	_____

Good parents should . . .	Agree	Maybe	Disagree
Play with and give generous hugs to their children.	_____	_____	_____
Not ask children to do anything that parents would not do.	_____	_____	_____
Eliminate harmful habits their children might copy.	_____	_____	_____
Never disagree in front of children.	_____	_____	_____
Spend some individual time with each child every day.	_____	_____	_____
Let children see how they resolve their own disagreements.	_____	_____	_____
On major decisions consult with each other before doing what a child asks.	_____	_____	_____
Other: _____	_____	_____	_____
Other: _____	_____	_____	_____

Through parenting, you choose the future by the ways you influence your children, both consciously and unconsciously. Children usually do what they see you do. They will probably model much of what they do on their experiences with and observations of you and your spouse.

As parents, you prepare your children for independent adult living from infancy. You share your love power as you gradually assist your children to take more and more responsibility for themselves. In these many ways children and adolescents learn how to make good decisions as they experience the consequences of decisions they make with your guidance.

Some ways my parents helped me to be independent and responsible: _____.

A situation when I was a child or adolescent and I discovered on my own that my parents were right: _____.

A situation when I was a child or adolescent and I found a better way to do something right: _____.

THE NEXT GENERATION 65

Each day's decisions and experiences contribute to a child's sense of love, acceptance, independence, and self-esteem. Through play, sports, hobbies, home activities, and many more encounters, parents demonstrate to their children how to act as adults.

> **P**
> **L O V E**
> **O**
> **W**
> **E**
> **R**
>
> *Train up a child in the way he should go,*
> *And when he is old he will not depart from*
> *it (Prov. 22:6–7).*

DECISIONS ABOUT YOUR CHILDREN

Your use of this section depends upon where you are in regard to children:

- Plan never to have children.
- Plan to have children at least one or two years from now.
- Plan to have children immediately.
- Already have some children, but plan to have more.
- Have all the children we ever plan to have.
- Other: _____

In answering and discussing these questions, adjust them to fit your situation. Do you and your spouse agree on the above category in which you place yourselves now? If not, find a way to agree and discuss your answers.

What I most enjoy about children: _____.

How I feel about having children: _____.

What effect or impact do (or will)
your children have on your marriage? _____

What good things happened to you as a child or adolescent that you also want to happen to your children?

Some things I want to do with or for my children: _____.

If you plan to have more children, you and your spouse must also make decisions about the number and spacing of children. These decisions then affect many other dimensions of parenting.

> **P**
> **L O V E**
> **W**
> **E**
> **R**
>
> *Consider what a different world we would have if the conception of every child were planned, and every child were wanted by a woman and a man who loved each other and knew how to create a secure and healthy home for that child, and did it.*

The spacing of children I prefer is _____.

This fits with our current family situation in these ways: _____.

Concerning whether we have boys or girls, I feel _____.

Our current conception control procedure is _____.

About this procedure, I feel _____.

About this procedure, my spouse feels _____.

Some more concerns I have
about children everywhere: _____.

Some more concerns I
have about parenting: _____.

Ways in which my choices about the future
are related to the next generation: _____.

Chapter 8

The World in Which You Live

"Wouldn't it be wonderful to run off to our own private place for another honeymoon?" Ingrid dreamed.

"Let's go," John responded. "Let's price an island or maybe a mountain retreat."

Continuing the fantasy, Ingrid slowly mused, "What do you want it to be like?"

"Well, first of all it includes you," John said as he gently coaxed her closer to him.

How would you complete this dialogue with your spouse? Perhaps one dream of every couple is to retreat to a beautiful island, beach house, or mountain cabin and honeymoon forever. This is a wonderful dream, which you may approximate at times in vacations and retreats. Yet every island is eventually part of the earth, and every couple is connected to others in many ways.

The world touches you through:

- the noise from the residents next door.
- the stranger who brought your lost pet back to you.
- the crowds that found your secret shortcut.
- the music and poetry that brighten each day.
- both the information and the garbage that TV delivers.

Although you may not control what happens, you can choose what impact or effects the events have on you. Here are some ways the world may affect you, your marriage, your home, and your community. Write examples of how each shows up in your life and how you choose to respond.

Crime: _____.

Schools: _____.

Community services: _____.

Police, emergency services: _____.

Noise, pollution: _____.

Neighbors: _____.

Television: _____.

Churches: _____.

Environmental issues: _____.

Federal or state debts and deficits: _____.

<blockquote>
P
L O V E
W
E
R

[The commandments] are all summed up in this saying, namely, "You shall love your neighbor as yourself." Love does no harm to a neighbor (Rom. 13:9-10).
</blockquote>

You choose how you want to affect the world. Here are ways that you can influence the world about you. Give an example of what you would do in each area and the results you hope would happen for others. For instance, you may give money to an agency to help feed hungry persons, or you may volunteer time to help in a hospital so others will feel hope and encouragement.

Helping neighbors: _____.

Political action: _____.

Church: _____.

Community: _____.

Schools: _____.

Emergency relief efforts: _____.

Environmental improvement: _____.

Others: _____.

Where I have invested myself with strength: _____.

Where I would like to invest my resources: _____.

FOLLOWING YOUR RAINBOW

Because rainbows usually occur when skies are clearing after a rain, the rainbow is often used as a sign of hope for the future. Having clear hope for tomorrow gives energy and anticipation to you and your spouse. Seeing possibilities enables you to express your best selves in all aspects of life. Hope affects what you do in your marriage, family, and occupation. Hope encourages you to work with friends, neighbors, church, and community.

Some rainbows of hope that I
want to share with my spouse are _____.

Colors I like for my life are _____.

Colors I dislike are _____.

Reasons for my choices are _____.

Ways I would like to change myself: _____.

Ways I would like to change my community: _____.

Ways I would like to change the world: _____.

Specific plans: _____.

Chapter 9

Careers

"It's impossible," lamented Fred.

"What's impossible?" Jan responded, picking up on her husband's frown.

"We are committed to put each other first, but I am also committed to put my profession first." Fred continued, "And you are also committed to putting your work first. Plus, there are the children. How do we put God first and still put these first?"

"We can fit these commitments together somehow," Jan assured him.

"A nice idea in theory," Fred replied. "Just how can we really put all of these first at the same time?"

We choose our future when we choose our faith, our partners, our children, and the world—the people of the neighborhood, city, state, and nation.

Your fifth choice about your future is your career or work. Through your work, you invest your time and energy in shaping the future. You can help others grow to and through healthy adulthood.

FINDING YOUR VOCATION OR CALLING

From a Christian perspective, vocation is a calling from God to make vocal one's faith through one's life. A career path is one way that you embody who you are through the world of work. Some would say that where the needs of the world and your talents meet, there is your possible calling.

When I think of my job, work, or career, I _____.

Some ways I have a calling or vocation are _____.

My calling may take me in several directions, such as _____.

My career is or will be _____.

I can use my paid work to benefit others in these ways: _____.

Your vocation involves your interests and skills in relation to the opportunities that you have to apply these skills and interests to life situations. You may become clearer about your vocation or calling as you observe others, such as relatives and friends, in the work that they do and their reactions to their work.

FAMILY OF ORIGIN INFLUENCES

Families provide models for success and often provide, as much as they can, some of the resources necessary for a given career choice.

Ways my family has helped me in my career decisions: _____.

Ways my family has limited me in my career decisions: _____.

EDUCATION

The type and amount of formal education and/or vocational training affect you in three major ways:

1. As preparation for living, education shapes your ability to acquire and evaluate information about any subject area.

2. As preparation for a career, education introduces you to the information and skills that you need to enter a career or the job market at the level you want.

3. As a social experience, education enables you to meet friends you would not otherwise have met. Since an educational setting brings together many persons who have in common a desire for self-improvement and learning (at least to some extent!), you may meet persons who will become lifelong friends because of common interests and concerns.

In what ways is each of these consequences of formal education a factor for you now? _____

If you are now in an educational setting, such as college or vocational training school, how do you feel about the experiences you are having? _____

Are you getting all that you want from your education? _____

If not, what is missing? _____

If you have completed your college,
professional, or vocational preparation, what
are the most valuable results that you have gained? _____
(*If you are now in college, imagine that you have
completed your education and are looking back at
the experience as you answer this question.*)

Could (or do) you combine education and marriage? _____

What special factors might be present in a
marriage if one or both partners are attending
college or professional school? _____

INTERACTIONS OF CAREER, MARRIAGE, AND FAITH

How do (or will) these career stages interact with other areas of your life? It may
help you to enter the approximate age when each stage might occur for you as
you compare where you might be in marriage, family, and other areas.

Career Stage	Age	Effects on Marriage	Relation to Faith
Preparation	_____	_____	_____
Entry	_____	_____	_____
Advancement	_____	_____	_____
Establishment	_____	_____	_____
Maintenance	_____	_____	_____
Reassessment	_____	_____	_____
Another career	_____	_____	_____
Retirement or reengagement	_____	_____	_____
Other stages	_____	_____	_____

Your confidence about controlling your career path depends upon your skills,
motivation, and initiative.

CAREER INTEREST DIMENSIONS

There are at least six major dimensions involved in choosing a career. When you
complete the questions and statements related to each dimension, you may have
a clearer idea of whether you are in the career path you want.

1. Interests

I enjoy doing these activities: _____.

I dislike very much these activities: _____.

What excites me most about life is _____.

If I did not need to worry about income, I would _____.

2. Abilities

I have these abilities: _____.

I can do these things well: _____.

I have succeeded in these activities: _____.

My best skills are _____.

3. Goals

My major long-range objectives for my life are _____.

Some short-range goals are _____.

In my life I would most like to accomplish _____.

4. Expectations of Others

What others expect or want me to do as a career is _____.

I cope with these expectations by _____.

Others control my choices by _____.

5. Opportunities

Society will pay me to maximize these
interests, goals, abilities, and expectations:_____.

These job opportunities are available for me: _____.

I can create a paying job for myself in these ways: _____.

6. Rewards

What rewards or results are important to you? _____

How important is each of the following?

• Doing something interesting: _____.
• Achieving a certain goal: _____.
• Making a lot of money: _____.
• Having job security: _____.

Of these, the most important for me is _____.

I will know I have received the rewards I want when _____.

After you have considered each dimension, discuss them with your partner.

SOME COMMON CLUSTERS OF WORK

Choosing your career or job involves values, interests, skills, opportunities, and resources. Consider these clusters of careers. Rate your interests and your skill level for each type of work. Ask your partner to rate these same dimensions.

	Husband's Answers			Wife's Answers		
	High	*Mid*	*Low*	*High*	*Mid*	*Low*
Agriculture and nature	____	____	____	____	____	____
Adventure	____	____	____	____	____	____
Military activities	____	____	____	____	____	____
Mechanical activities	____	____	____	____	____	____
Basic science and math	____	____	____	____	____	____
Medical services	____	____	____	____	____	____
Music, drama, performing arts	____	____	____	____	____	____
Visual arts, advertising	____	____	____	____	____	____
Teaching	____	____	____	____	____	____
Social services	____	____	____	____	____	____
Athletics, sports	____	____	____	____	____	____
Homemaking and child rearing	____	____	____	____	____	____
Religious activities	____	____	____	____	____	____
Public speaking	____	____	____	____	____	____

	Husband's Answers			Wife's Answers		
	High	Mid	Low	High	Mid	Low
Law, politics	___	___	___	___	___	___
Merchandising	___	___	___	___	___	___
Sales	___	___	___	___	___	___
Business management	___	___	___	___	___	___
Office practices	___	___	___	___	___	___
Other: _____	___	___	___	___	___	___

After both have created the profiles, talk about how your choices express your faith, your commitment to each other, your concern about the next generations, and your relationship with other persons.

Three major components of life are education, work, and leisure. All three relate directly to your marriage.

Education involves decisions about life goals and career directions. Education for a physician, minister, attorney, teacher, or other profession requires many years and much money. One's educational program will probably determine where a couple lives, income level, and the time spouses will have together.

My plans concerning
preparation for vocation: _____

_____.

Career has direct and constant impact on marriage. Some spouses may prefer an eight-to-five job with regular hours and little financial risk, while others seek careers that have very demanding schedules, high financial risk, and much emotional strain. When spouses differ on their career styles and interests, they must work together to create solutions.

My plans concerning work and career: _____

_____.

Where I have ventured in spite of my limits: _____

_____.

Leisure is both quality and quantity of time available after work is done. Spouses must choose how much time to be with each other and how much to be involved in individual activities.

My plans concerning volunteer work and leisure:_____

_____.

CHOICES I NOW MAKE CONCERNING THE FUTURE

In Part 2, we've discussed each of the following elements. Take some time to jot down additional ideas or reminders to yourself about your choices. You may want to discuss the whole subject of choosing your future with your spouse at this time.

Personal faith, choosing the
life given to me: _____

_____

Commitment, vows, promises to my spouse: _____

_____

My relationship with children,
the next generation: _____

_____

World—neighbors, community,
society, environment: _____

_____

Careers—implementing dreams and visions for the future: _____

_____

Part 3

INCREASING YOUR POSITIVES

Multiplying your good times

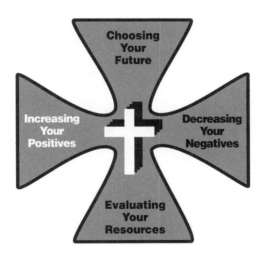

Positives are your skills for achieving your goals, maintaining the lifestyle patterns you want, and having fun. Having effective skills for increasing your positive patterns of care and mutually beneficial actions will also crowd out any negatives.

Think of some good skills you already have, such as _____.

Some skills we, as a couple, plan
to use to achieve our goals are _____.

The skills I like best are _____.

The skills my spouse likes best are _____.

Chapter 10

Affection and the Sexual Relationship

"It feels so good when you hold me," Paula whispered to her husband, Mike. "Like being completely safe and absolutely certain nothing can hurt me."

"I'm glad you like it," replied Mike. "I like holding you, and I like it when you reach out and hold me."

"Just one of the many ways I enjoy being with you," continued Paula.

"And I really appreciate you in more ways every day," confided Mike as he snuggled into her arms.

Affection and intimacy expand sexual activities into channels for meaningful love. Sex and touch are based in the brain, which controls the neurological networks for social and sexual intercourse.

P
L O V E
W
E
R

When things go right, we know what we can do next time so we can increase our skills for love.

TOUCHES FROM YOUR PAST

The word *feel* can refer either to touch or to emotions. Emotions are closely related to touch experiences. Through good touch experiences, you learn to feel good about yourself and your body.

Many of the meanings you have attached to touch come out of your past. These meanings influence how you feel about touch, sex, and other intimacies in your marriage.

How and where did you learn
your standards for touching others? _____

Touch helps me to feel
closer to others in my family by _____.

When did touch cause you to feel
afraid of others in your family? _____

You give meaning to physical contact between you and another person. You can be touched or not touched, and each can be good or bad. Thus there are always four possibilities concerning whether to touch or not, to be touched or not. These possibilities change according to how you perceive the other person involved.

	Good	*Bad*
Touched	Affirmed Accepted Comforted	Invaded Controlled Abused
Not touched	Free Flexible Respected	Isolated Lonely Forgotten

TOUCH AND SEX

Experiences with touch greatly affect your sexuality since touch is part of sex.

God has created the complex chemistry of sexual reproduction in wonderful and magnificent ways, yet God allows you to choose how you will use your sexuality. To your spouse, you can choose to express affirmation, affection, care, love, tenderness, acceptance, life, and union through sexuality.

Times when I am most aware of love and
affirmation in my sexual expressions are_____.

Glances, sounds, hugs, kisses, words, silence—all can convey affirmation in many ways. Through them, you are nourished, and through them, you nourish your partner.

It is a thrill to receive from my spouse
these expressions of love: _____.

TALKING WITH TOUCH

One wife said, "When I ask my husband if he loves me, he thinks I'm asking for information. I want action, not information."

Endearing terms and "I love you" statements have deeper meaning when you and your spouse have an emotional bank account of many good hugs, kisses, and other positive touch patterns. Words point to actions, and actions validate words.

My actions validate my words in these ways: _____.

My words point to my actions in these ways: _____.

To show affection means to show love and care for another person as God loves you. Affection is the major nutrient in healthy families. Here are some benefits of giving and receiving affection. In each space describe a situation when you were especially aware of that benefit.

Helped to heal old hurts: _____.

Strengthened self-esteem: _____.

Fulfilled personal hungers
for acceptance and attention: _____.

Was fun to do because healthy
love gives pleasure to both the
receiver and the giver: _____.

Forgave the other person: _____.

Find an appropriate time with your spouse when you can practice exchanging loving touches. Face each other, hold hands, and give your appreciation to your spouse in both words and touch. Then be open to receiving a similar affirmation from your spouse. Each time reply with a warm "thank you" and a hug.

SOME SEX PATTERNS

The human sexual intercourse cycle has four primary phases: (1) *excitement* (getting turned on to sex with your spouse), (2) *plateau* (intense excitement continues at a high level), (3) *orgasm* (a varied pattern of intense muscular contractions), (4) *resolution* (gradual return to usual unexcited levels).

Sexual interest, desires, and energy vary in the same person at different times and under different conditions. General health, stress, conflicts, and many other factors influence each person's sensitivity to sexual stimuli and patterns of sexual response.

Times when I am most sexually interested are _____.

Times when my spouse is most sexually interested are _____.

How often do you want sexual intercourse to occur in your marriage? _____

Differences in sexual cycles,
attitudes, and expectations that
my spouse and I can change are _____.

Warm romantic touches I enjoy from my spouse include _____.

Warm romantic touches I like to give to my spouse include _____.

SEXUAL ATTITUDES AFFECT INTIMACY

How does each partner feel about sexuality? What sexual behaviors do you most enjoy? Which sexual activities do you dislike or find distasteful? How do you feel about sexual relations with your spouse?

How I feel about our sexual relationship: _____.

How do you express your affection for your spouse through sexual ways? Does your spouse recognize these as expressions of affection or merely as attempts to have sex for your pleasure only?

Some meanings of sexual activities for us are _____.

Here are a series of personal questions about your sexual relationship in your marriage. You may prefer not to write in answers to some of them, or you may use the blank lines to make notes for you and your spouse to discuss.

What type of contraception method(s) do (or will) you use in your marriage? Whose decision is this? What are the advantages and disadvantages of the method(s)? How are sexual activities related to your plans to have or not to have children? Are both you and your spouse satisfied with your method(s)?

_____

_____

_____

EXPRESSING CARE AND AFFECTION

Expressing positive feelings between you and your spouse is the primary bond that maintains your common lifestyle together.

Positive sexual feelings include love, care, concern, happiness, and pleasure, among others.

What words or phrases describe
your positive sexual feelings?_____

You can express positive feelings of care and affection in many ways: smiling, touching, being on time, scheduling time together, praising your partner for words and actions that are meaningful to you, and helping your partner accomplish goals.

Describe three specific ways you express care and affection to your spouse:

1. _____.
2. _____.
3. _____.

Describe three specific ways that your spouse expresses care and affection to you:

1. _____.
2. _____.
3. _____.

How do sexual activities relate to other ways that you give care and affection to each other?

Good sex relates to _____.

Laughter and humor are often parts of genuine affection. Describe the most recent time you and your partner laughed heartily together, at no one's expense.

A time when laughter added to my sexual enjoyment was _____.

P
L O V E
W
E
R

Wives, love your husbands, and "husbands, love your wives, just as Christ also loved the church and gave Himself for her" (Eph. 5:25).

When you and your spouse care deeply for each other, you are able to use touching and sexual activities to enhance your intimacy and joyous quality times together. You can talk openly about what you like and do not like. In love you can find ways to continue to express warmth and affirmation. This freedom helps your sex life improve, also.

You cannot keep love. You can only give love to others. In return you receive the blessing of growing in your love for your spouse and for all.

Chapter 11

Money and Financial Issues

"How will we ever be able to pay all our bills, save some money, give some, and still do what we want for our family?" groaned Bob as he sat balancing the checkbook.

Putting her arms around Bob's shoulders, Sue slowly replied, "It takes work and planning and determination and . . ."

Smiling at her, Bob caught her warmth. "I know, I know. It's just that I had hoped we could be farther ahead financially than we now are."

"So did I," agreed Sue, "yet we will find ways to make it somehow. Let's talk about some possibilities. Money or not, I still love you."

Money is not the root of all evil. It is the *love of money* that produces evil. Money is the major way modern society translates work and power into an exchange medium so that we can more easily trade resources with others.

Money has many meanings, from having enough dollars to pay bills to imparting status and power.

To me, money means _____.

CHARITABLE CONTRIBUTIONS

Charitable contributions are a major way you share your financial blessings with others. The biblical concept of tithing means that you set up a percentage of your income (such as 10 percent) to share with others.

What are some needs to which you contribute or want to contribute? How can your gifts help to feed, house, clothe, or educate people?

I would like to contribute this amount each week, month, or year: _____.

The amount I want to give to my church is _____.

I want to contribute to these agencies: _____.

As stewards of God's blessings to us, we want
to give some contributions to these causes: _____.

When I contribute to my church and other
agencies that help others, I feel _____.

SAVINGS AND EMERGENCIES

By setting a specific amount to save each week, month, or year, you can build a fund for emergencies, future purchases, vacations, and retirement. You will have more options and greater flexibility when you are faced with home or automobile repairs, a job termination, or other unexpected expenses.

The amount I would like to save is _____.

BUDGETARY SKILLS

There are at least two types of skills you need to manage your money so that your money doesn't manage your marriage.

The Treasurer or Accounting Function

In your marriage, which partner is responsible for paying bills, writing checks, keeping up with charge accounts, and maintaining records of expenditures? Which one likes to do this (or dislikes doing it less)? One of you may do most of the bookkeeping, or each may do parts of it according to time and interests.

The treasurer for our marriage is _____.

The Executive or Decision Function

Regardless of who is the treasurer, both partners need to be in agreement about money, income, and expenses before they happen. Among possible arrangements are mutual, joint decisions on most or all items, one spouse decides on most or all items, or each spouse pays certain items.

The decision arrangement that is
best for us in our marriage is _____.

Separate clearly the treasurer function from the executive or decision function concerning the uses of your money. Sometimes it is easy to assume that the person writing the checks automatically has final say over how money is spent.

How I feel about our money arrangements: _____.

How my spouse feels about our money arrangements: _____.

What type of checking, savings, credit card, and other money management methods do you use in your marriage? Do you agree on them? How do you want to change them?

_____

_____

The executive function refers to how you make decisions about your money and finances. If you do not already have the following elements in place, make notes about how you can use each in the budget and financial planning for your marriage.

A regular time each week or month
when we can discuss our finances is _____.

When a financial problem or urgent money matter occurs, we _____.

Some special expense concerns we must solve soon are _____.

We handle indebtedness and abuses of our credit by _____.

We do not want to owe more than _____.

Ways we are, or plan to be, financially sound are _____.

My concerns about buying on credit are _____.

YOUR BASIC SPENDING PLAN OR BUDGET

With your spouse, consider the total amount of money you have each month. Begin with the total amount, then subtract taxes and other fixed expenses.

Listed here are most basic spending categories. Allocate your income to these categories. As you consider the ways you use your income and money, keep aware of your feelings and perhaps conflicts that may arise.

It will help you stabilize your monthly or weekly money needs by dividing your annual income by twelve (months) to show how much per month you have available.

Our Income	*Annual*	*Monthly*
From wife's career or job	_____	_____
From husband's career or job	_____	_____
From other sources (explain)	_____	_____
Totals	_____	_____

Our Expenses	*Annual*	*Monthly*
Taxes and Social Security	_____	_____
Emergency	_____	_____
Contributions (religious, charitable)	_____	_____
Housing and utilities	_____	_____
Food (includes eating out)	_____	_____
Health, medical, insurance	_____	_____
Clothing	_____	_____
Personal fund for wife	_____	_____
Personal fund for husband	_____	_____
Dues, professional, work expenses	_____	_____
Transportation expenses (auto, etc.)	_____	_____
Installment payments (for:_____)	_____	_____
Education	_____	_____
Savings and investments	_____	_____
Children	_____	_____
Leisure and recreation	_____	_____
Other: _____	_____	_____
Other: _____	_____	_____
Other: _____	_____	_____
Totals	_____	_____

Regardless of your age or your financial assets, you ought to have at least a simple will that will convey the executor functions to your spouse in case of your death. You may consult with an attorney about details of a will.

Does either spouse have property or other financial resources that you will want to continue as separate property so that it does not become involved with the community property of your marriage?

If your state has community property laws, have you made the necessary provisions to give appropriate legal status to any property you want to keep separate from your marriage? Consult an attorney concerning the best ways to ensure that these resources continue legally separate for you.

Concerning separate property, we will _____.

About having legally separate property, I feel _____.

Ways my will and other legal documents protect
the legal interests of my spouse and others,
such as children from a previous marriage, are _____.

SOME CHOICES CONCERNING FINANCES AND MONEY

Here are several financial and budget issues that most couples face. Write in how you will handle each topic, and then discuss your answers with your spouse.

Charge cards: _____

Writing checks: _____

Setting up a budget: _____

Savings and investments: _____

Major purchases: _____

Property (house, car): _____

Separate property: _____

Will, living trust: _____

Husband's income: _____

Wife's income: _____

Gifts and contributions: _____

_____ : _____

_____ : _____

Some ways we now use our money and financial resources that I like and want to keep are_____.

Some ways we now use our money and financial resources that I don't like and don't want to keep are_____.

P
L O V E
W
E
R

Positive actions move you toward the future you want.

Chapter 12

Lifestyle Patterns

"It sure gets tedious," murmured Leo as he put on his sweats for his workout at the gym.

"What's tedious, Leo?" answered Juan from across the way.

"Oh, I like to watch the football games, but Maria has her study table next to the TV, and she complains that she can't concentrate with the TV blasting."

Laughing a bit, Juan challenged, "Have you ever thought about moving either the TV or the study table?"

"Hey, maybe that's our answer!" Leo exclaimed. "I wonder if Maria would be open to that?"

Meanwhile on the jogging trail, Maria and Anna are talking as they jog.

Maria, a bit sad, comments, "I wish Leo would be more open to changing our furniture around. He's just like his dad that way."

"Meaning what?" inquired Anna.

"Oh, I'd like to move my study table into our bedroom, away from the TV. When the TV is going, I can't focus on my classwork."

After a bit, Anna asked, "What does Leo want to do?"

"I don't know. He probably wants things to stay as they are." Catching her breath, Maria continued, "Come to think of it, I'm not sure we ever talked about this. I certainly want to, but I . . ."

Later that evening when Maria and Leo are at home, what do you think happened? Write the next statement that each of them might make, or write the statements you and your spouse might make in a similar situation.

Lifestyle patterns refer to the many habits and routines that you use every day, either as individuals or as a couple. These include the amount of privacy and rules for its use, activity, cleanliness (or its lack!), type of residence and automobile, how to use home furnishings, and many more elements.

Each partner brings background, interests, interpersonal skills, habits, goals, and commitments to the marriage. Recognizing the uniqueness of each partner allows both of you to blend your lives together so that you continue to be unique individuals and also learn to work and play together as a couple.

> **P**
> **L O V E**
> **W**
> **E**
> **R**
>
> *Good marriages are not made in heaven. A good marriage comes in a kit, and you and your spouse have to put it together. Sometimes parts don't fit, and you have to improvise and try again.*

Common tasks are regularly recurring activities in which partners are involved together. Too often, "common" refers to insignificant, boring, or unimportant. However, the tasks included in this chapter are at the heart of the relationship between two partners.

Your schedules and activities involve your daily interactions with each other. Some of these daily activities may involve other persons in addition to your spouse.

Concerning our daily activities, I feel _____.

About these, I think my partner feels _____.

A change in expectations I would like to have is _____.

LIVING AREA

In many ways your residential or living area is an extension of you. You may have little interest in details of your residence, or you may consider it to be very important. You and your spouse may agree or disagree about which details are important and should be done a certain way.

Do you rent or lease? Or are you buying your residence? _____

What are the advantages and disadvantages of this? _____

What do you like about your floor plan, furniture,
and home arrangements? _____

How is your home arranged to maximize
convenience and minimize conflicts? _____

What do you like best about your home? Why? _____

What are the disadvantages of your home?
Why are they disadvantages? _____

In which room do you spend most time? _____

In which room do you spend least time? _____

Which room is most difficult to keep clean? _____

Who is responsible for keeping each room in order? _____

How much closet, drawer, and
storage space do you need? _____

What are your other concerns about your home? _____

SOME DAILY BASICS

Here are some aspects of lifestyle that may or may not be important to you and/or to your partner. For each item, mark the column that shows how you evaluate it.

	Not Important	Somewhat Important	Very Important	Absolutely Essential
Personal privacy	_____	_____	_____	_____
Mealtime activity (talking, TV)	_____	_____	_____	_____
When to go to sleep and get up	_____	_____	_____	_____
Home temperature (day/night)	_____	_____	_____	_____
Television programs and videos	_____	_____	_____	_____
Geographical area where we live	_____	_____	_____	_____
Size and style of our home	_____	_____	_____	_____

	Not Important	Somewhat Important	Very Important	Absolutely Essential
Details of furniture and interior decorating	_____	_____	_____	_____
Devotional, prayer times	_____	_____	_____	_____
Other: _____	_____	_____	_____	_____

Exploring these areas can be exciting, enjoyable, and renewing. Knowing what you want or expect and being clear about what you are willing to give and do expand your opportunities for joy and happiness together.

If you have tension around some areas of disagreement, pause, back off a bit, laugh at how you may be making a mountain out of a molehill, and then express the positive facets of your daily lives together. Exchange a hug.

You may need to postpone difficult disagreements. Later, when you are ready, you can apply the problem-solving and conflict resolution steps from Part 6 to these more difficult topics. Your common experiences of joy and care for each other strengthen you for resolving these disagreements.

An area of disagreement is _____.

The way we plan to work on this is _____.

Regardless of where we are living,
I want our home to be a place where we can _____.

Most of our decisions about
our residence should be made by   both_____   wife_____   husband_____.

We will make these decisions by _____.

SCHEDULES, ROUTINES, AND TIME USE

Whether you have a formalized schedule or not, you have habits, routines, and patterns for your married life. For example, you know the amount of time it takes for you to get up and get going each day. If your spouse needs about the same amount of time, you may have many unspoken agreements about use of the bathroom, breakfast, closet access, television, exercise, showers, devotionals, and the other details of getting ready for work or leisure.

Stress results when your patterns conflict. Many little unnoticed stresses can add up to a general feeling of uneasiness, pressure, or discomfort. When you agree on patterns that allow flexibility, hugs, and tender moments as well as accomplish your goals, you build positive deposits in your emotional banks. Routines then become fun and freeing for both of you.

For me, daily schedules mean _____.

The part of the day or week
when I feel most stressed is _____.

The part of the day or week
when I feel most relaxed is _____.

I am able to give my spouse silent time for _____.

Our times for spiritual renewal are _____.

Some special times in our marriage are _____.

Patterns we practice in our marriage are _____.

PERSONAL HABITS AND CHARACTERISTICS

Some qualities and characteristics may be more important or less important in your daily marriage activities. Identifying your agreements and differences on these details can enable you to appreciate each other as you learn to be more open and honest in your caring and love.

For each, place a check mark in the blank to show how important it is for you. You may invite your spouse to use a different color or symbol to show preferences. Then compare and discuss your answers with your spouse.

	Not Important	Somewhat Important	Very Important	Absolutely Essential
Intelligence	_____	_____	_____	_____
Similar values, interests	_____	_____	_____	_____
Intimacy, closeness	_____	_____	_____	_____
Agreements about roles	_____	_____	_____	_____
Troublesome differences	_____	_____	_____	_____
Energy level	_____	_____	_____	_____
Personal habits	_____	_____	_____	_____
Use of money	_____	_____	_____	_____
Verbal skills, interests	_____	_____	_____	_____
Flexibility, adaptability	_____	_____	_____	_____
Response style (fast/slow)	_____	_____	_____	_____

	Not Important	Somewhat Important	Very Important	Absolutely Essential
Affection, nurture	_____	_____	_____	_____
Spontaneous, exciting	_____	_____	_____	_____
Quiet, thoughtful	_____	_____	_____	_____
Personality	_____	_____	_____	_____
Appearance	_____	_____	_____	_____
Ambition, drive	_____	_____	_____	_____
Character, integrity	_____	_____	_____	_____
Creativity, doing new things	_____	_____	_____	_____
Parenting, children issues	_____	_____	_____	_____
Authenticity, being real	_____	_____	_____	_____
Self-confidence, self-esteem	_____	_____	_____	_____
Openness, honesty	_____	_____	_____	_____
Sense of humor, laughter	_____	_____	_____	_____
Punctuality	_____	_____	_____	_____
Dependability, trust	_____	_____	_____	_____

P
L O V E
O
W
E
R

The ways you do the many daily details of marriage dramatize how you really value each other. Daily living is your faith in action.

Chapter 13

Health and Well-Being

A holistic health view means that all aspects of your health have physical, psychological, and spiritual dimensions. Physical aspects include the structure of your body, your biochemical and hormonal balances, and your genetic factors. Your psychological dimension includes your emotional reactions, mental abilities, and personality dimensions. Spiritual aspects include your self-image, attitudes, values, and faith perspectives.

These dimensions always work in combination within you. For example, a person may have a physical illness, which is made worse by becoming depressed or by feeling guilty or ashamed. On the other hand, with the same physical illness another person may feel very confident of recovery because of trust that God's healing is being experienced through medical care.

There is much evidence that good health and a positive lifestyle are related. Good health gives energy and pleasure, which contribute to increased stamina and persistence. In turn, willpower brings patience, hope, and happiness.

Ways that health and happiness are related are _____.

Positive attitudes and appropriate
body care contribute to better
physical and mental health through_____.

Your body is a temple of God. As a temple of God, you can embody God's spirit of love and power to your spouse and to others.

When I consider my body as a temple of
God, I mean _____.

Preventive medical checkups are wise moves because _____.

Habits I have stopped (or will stop)
to improve my health are _____.

HEALTH AND MARRIAGE

A satisfying marriage with warmth, openness, flexibility, and support contributes much to your health. Good health contributes to marital happiness by improving sexual energy and performance, freeing you to focus on work and leisure interests, and reducing the amount of time and money you must spend on health treatments.

Our health and marriage quality are
related in these ways: _____ .

The ways I use each of these to maintain good health:

Exercise: _____ .

Diet: _____ .

Mealtimes: _____ .

Sleep: _____ .

Daily habits: _____ .

Stress reduction: _____ .

Other: _____ .

P
L O V E
W
E
R

Your body is the temple of the Holy Spirit who is in you, whom you have from God. . . . Therefore glorify God in your body and in your spirit, which are God's (1 Cor. 6:19-20).

HEALTH CHALLENGES

Every person has some physical challenges, some more severe than others.

My physical disabilities or limitations are _____ .

My spouse's physical disabilities or limitations are _____ .

My feelings about them are _____ .

Treatments that help these conditions are _____ .

Health science advances have provided treatments and helps for many health dysfunctions, yet there are other conditions for which we have not yet found causes, cures, and related treatment.

If you or your spouse has a health condition for which there is no treatment known, how do you feel about this? _____

If treatments are available for your condition, how do you feel about the cost, time, and/or uncomfortable aspects? _____

HEALTH CONCERNS

Which of the following might be a health concern or problem for you in your marriage? After both answer, discuss your findings with your spouse.

	No Problem	Might Be a Problem	Big Problem
When to see a physician	_____	_____	_____
Health insurance	_____	_____	_____
Weight and diet	_____	_____	_____
Heart condition	_____	_____	_____
Cancer	_____	_____	_____
AIDS, HIV virus	_____	_____	_____
Smoking	_____	_____	_____
Alcohol, other drugs	_____	_____	_____
Diabetes	_____	_____	_____
Physical disabilities	_____	_____	_____
Hearing or vision	_____	_____	_____
Exercise	_____	_____	_____
Depression	_____	_____	_____
Unpredictable moods	_____	_____	_____
Intellectual ability	_____	_____	_____
Cleanliness: house, clothes	_____	_____	_____
Personal body hygiene	_____	_____	_____
Ways of handling sickness	_____	_____	_____
Health standards	_____	_____	_____

ILLNESS AND CHRONIC CONDITIONS

Among other interpretations, illness can be considered a signal to a person that something has gone wrong in the human (body-mind-spirit) system. Illness may bring permanent changes (or damages) that mean a person must adjust to a permanent or chronic condition of reduced physical activity.

Consider illnesses and other health problems or concerns you have had in the past or now have.

What is your interpretation of illness? _____

    Is illness the result of specific physical
    conditions that affect the body and mind? _____

    Is illness purely physical? _____

    Is health merely the absence of illness, or
    is illness an interruption of good health? _____

To what extent can (or do) you choose to be sick or well? _____

Physical illnesses I have had: _____.

Physical illnesses family members have had: _____.

My reactions or feelings about them: _____.

How they affect our marriage now: _____.

Which health conditions do you and/or
your spouse have that might be inherited
(or have been inherited) by your children? _____

To cope with these conditions I have received
this information and counseling: _____.

> P
> L O V E
> W
> E
> R
>
> *Let us lay aside every weight, and the sin which so easily ensnares us, and let us run with endurance the race that is set before us (Heb. 12:1).*

What plans, such as health insurance or
savings, do you have to assist you in coping
with illness and unexpected health concerns? _____

ACCIDENTS

You probably cope easily with minor accidents, but some accidents involve major
or permanent damage to persons or property. An accident also becomes a crisis if
you are not able to cope successfully with its consequences.

In recent months or years, accidents
that have happened to me or my family are _____.

If someone else has caused an accident that has bad results for you, how do you
feel about that person or group?

My feelings about those who caused this accident are _____.

When I am accidentally hurt, I most appreciate
my spouse doing these things to help me: _____.

If you have caused an accident that has bad results for your spouse (and/or for
others), how do you feel as a result?

About accidentally causing harm to someone else, I feel _____.

I am now doing these things to cope with my feelings
about my part in this accident: _____.

DEATH

Your perspectives on death grow out of your interpretation of life and the place
of death as part of living.

For me, death means _____.

How my faith gives meaning to death: _____.

I have experienced death in these ways: _____.

Relatives or friends who died include _____

My reactions to their deaths were _____.

Factors that helped me cope were _____.

Factors that made death worse for me were _____.

Was each death unexpected or the result of an extended illness? _____

How do you feel about your death? _____

Have you experienced any time
when you thought you might die? _____

My reactions to that near death situation were _____.

God helps me face death by _____.

You can help others deal better with your death in several ways, such as providing a will, insurance benefits, and other arrangements in case you should die unexpectedly.

What preparations have you made
to assist others in dealing with your death? _____

A living will is a way that a person can direct that his/her life not be sustained by artificial means when there is no hope of regaining normal functioning. There are many complex aspects related to when you or your spouse would choose to die rather than continue in a coma or with unbearable pain. You may explore these with your pastor, physician, or attorney.

Some ways I want to change to maintain
and improve my health are _____.

Some patterns I want to keep that help
me to maintain good health are _____.

Chapter 14

Leisure, Intimacy, and Fun Times

"I wish we had more time to play," Jim whispered in Judy's ear as he hugged her before she left for work.

"So do I," she answered, squeezing his hand again.

"How about this weekend?" he asked.

"Oh, yes! Let's dream of the possibilities, and tonight we can make some specific plans," suggested Judy.

"Sounds great to me, too," Jim agreed as they parted for work.

After the time required for your jobs, you and your spouse decide how you will spend the remaining time available to you. You will probably spend some of this time together, and some of your time, whether together or separate, will be spent in leisure, community, and recreational activities.

Leisure, community, and recreational interests enable you to develop other facets of yourself in addition to those related to your career.

INDIVIDUAL PERSONAL TIME

How do you and your spouse divide your leisure time between individual interests (or personal leisure time) and joint couple interests (or couple together time)? Positive growth involves some of each.

How much leisure time should be
personal time for you and your spouse
to do things separately as individuals? _____

Things I like to do alone are _____.

You and your spouse may be able to schedule some personal or individual time by each doing your activities during the same time period. For example, both of you may have the same weeknight out so that neither feels left behind when the other is doing something enjoyable.

Some ways we schedule (or could schedule)
individual leisure activities at the same time: _____.

You or your spouse may enjoy more (or less) personal leisure time than the other does. Sometimes one spouse is involved in interesting, exciting activities that the other spouse does not like or would like to do but cannot.

What do you think of your spouse's leisure activities? _____

What does your spouse think of your leisure activities? _____

This attitude influences me and/or my spouse in these ways: _____.

I feel left out of the exciting activities of my spouse when _____.

I would like to (or will) change this by _____.

I would like to change the way in which
either or both of us use our leisure time by _____.

COUPLE LEISURE TIME

Mutually enjoyable activities bring fun, affirmation, and new experiences to renew your romance and enrich your marriage in many ways. These activities may be special dates, such as dinner out, movies, theater, sports events, and trips. They may be fun things you do alone as a couple or with others.

Activities we enjoy doing together are _____.

An activity I like that I want my spouse to participate in is _____.

An activity my spouse likes that I am
willing to participate in is _____.

Recreation that we like to do with others is _____.

As a couple, we plan to do more _____.

MAINTENANCE AND REPAIR TIMES

In addition to the obviously fun times, you probably have to devote some leisure time to maintaining your residence and automobile and taking care of other related home tasks. Doing dishes or laundry, housecleaning, lawn mowing, or making repairs may not seem like much fun, yet must be done. However, you and your spouse can often make these work times more pleasant by doing them together and including opportunities for quick talks, hugs, or refreshments.

Some ways we can make routine housework more fun are _____.

An unpleasant task neither of us likes to do is _____.

One way we could make this fun is _____.

Maintenance times refer also to maintaining your relationship with each other. If one spouse expects the other to do most of the unpleasant, boring, or routine jobs around the home, both miss the opportunity to work together, encourage each other, and talk more casually about anything and everything as you do the jobs.

For example, you can be thankful for having a home you can call your own (thus needing cleaning), for food to cook and eat (thus dirty dishes), and for some income (although perhaps not enough) with which to pay for basic needs.

Some changes we can make to reduce or
eliminate some of the unpleasant work at home are _____.

We can work together to do an unpleasant job by _____.

Is there only one way something must be done? Or are there several ways that could work to achieve the same goal? Being flexible about how you do things in your marriage allows for your individual differences.

We are flexible in these ways: _____.

SOME LEISURE FOR COMMUNITY SERVICE

Community involvement includes activities that make your community a better place in which to live: serving on civic committees, leading activities for children or youths in a community or religious organization, working in political campaigns.

In which activities are you involved now,
or do you want to become involved? _____

What causes do you work for, such
as environmental concerns, alternate
energy sources, or health concerns? _____

How much money do you give to benefit
others? What percentage of your income is it? _____

How does your volunteer work benefit children,
youths, older people, or other groups? _____

SOME LEISURE FOR RE-CREATING YOURSELF

Recreation may include hobbies, athletics, group or individual activities, travel,
reading, and artistic pursuits. Recreation refers to the ways in which you re-create
and renew yourself.

For recreation, I most enjoy _____.

Recreation I like to do alone: _____.

Recreation I enjoy with my spouse: _____.

Recreation I like to do with others: _____.

LEISURE AND INTIMACY: WHAT TO TALK ABOUT

Sometimes couples avoid leisure time together because they are uncomfortable
talking with each other.

Intimacy is much more than just sexual activities. There are dozens of topics that
you can use to increase intimacy with your spouse. The key is your willingness to
make it safe for your partner to say anything about any topic or feeling without
being criticized, rejected, or put down. To increase your intimacy, your spouse
must also make it safe for you to say what you think, feel, or want without fear of
being hurt or rejected.

Ways I try to make "talk times" safe for my spouse: _____.

Ways my spouse makes talk safe for me: _____.

There are at least four levels of intimate talk. You can talk together about others
(world issues, friends, relatives, children), about your spouse, about yourself, and
about your relationship. Check these levels together.

Level 1: Safe Talk About Other Things, Situations, Persons, and Events

These matter-of-fact statements have little room for opinion or evaluation. You
can talk about:

- something both know about, such as a ball game, play, movie, television, music, books, school event, work event, or news event.
- activities others did or will do, such as a social, party, hobby, or sport.
- new information about common interests, such as antique cars, sewing, gourmet cooking, space travel, airplanes, gardening, fishing, hiking, travel, or vacations.
- who, what, where, when, why, how (the basic reporter's questions) applied to any of these topics.

Possible topics for us to discuss are _____.

Persons we both like to talk about are _____.

Level 2: Talk About My Spouse

If you are willing to accept whatever the other person says without questioning it, criticizing it, or commenting on whether it is good or bad, you can probably enable your partner to continue talking for a long time.

Ask your partner some of these questions, and listen without comment to the answers. You can enter some notes in the blanks.

What do you like or dislike about something, such as any of the topics in Level 1?

_____

Concerning any activity or personal interest: When do you do it, how do you get ready, how did you learn about it, what has been the best time you did it, when were you most scared or surprised, and what do you most enjoy or dislike about it?

_____

What is most difficult, unique, expensive, or demanding about the topic or activity? How do or have you overcome these blocks to doing the activity?

_____

Avoid questions that can be answered with a simple yes or no. For example, instead of asking, "Is it fun?" try, "What is most fun about it?"

_____

After a few minutes, summarize what your partner has said and feed it back to see if you are understanding accurately. Then continue listening to the rest of the story.

_____

Level 3: Talk About Me

This is riskier because you are likely to be concerned about what the other person thinks about you and what the reaction will be. You can begin this level by asking your spouse to take some time to let you talk about what is going on inside you.

This is what I like or dislike about something,
such as any of the topics in Level 1: _____.

When I do it (the activity or topic), how I get ready, how I learned to
do it, the time I had most fun doing it, the time I was most surprised,
puzzled, scared, or exhausted doing it, and what I most enjoy or dislike
about doing it: _____.

My opinions, likes, criticisms, or evaluations about
events, activities, hobbies, sports, and other events: _____.

Check occasionally to be sure your partner wants to hear more
about your experiences and views. I try to be aware that my spouse
is still listening by _____.

Level 4: Talk About Us

This is riskiest because disclosing information your partner did not know may cause your spouse to withdraw.

What I think, feel, want, or hope for us as a
couple and/or as individuals in our marriage: _____.

What we do that I like or dislike
or would like to change or continue: _____.

Opinions, feelings, reactions, or
hopes about anything we do as a couple: _____.

Requests for changes that you want your
spouse to make, perhaps offered with your
willingness to make changes your spouse would like: _____.

May your marriage be a blessing to you and to all. May you laugh with joy as you savor the beauty of life. May your times together and times apart expand your visions and warm your heart.

Chapter 15

Celebrations, Friends, and Relatives

Celebrating with acquaintances and relatives gives you important social support systems. Your fun times may often include friends or relatives.

Celebrations may be holidays, birthdays, anniversaries, and other turning points in your lives. Where do you celebrate holidays, birthdays, and other special occasions? At your own home as a couple or at your in-laws' home? Maybe you celebrate more with friends than with family.

Consider some of these aspects of celebrations, friends, and relatives. Which ones are working well for you? Which ones do you need or want to modify, change, or stop?

WAYS I CELEBRATE LIFE

Ways I like to celebrate major holidays: _____.

I like to see my in-laws (*for example, weekly, monthly, annually, never*) _____.

My spouse likes to see my relatives
(*for example, weekly, monthly, annually, never*) _____.

Topics I enjoy discussing with these relatives: _____.

Topics I always avoid with these relatives: _____.

Ways I value and update my interpersonal and social skills: _____.

Birthday celebrations I enjoy: _____.

Ways we celebrate the arrival of a baby
in our extended family: _____.

Celebrations also help us to cope with losing relatives or friends because of death, moves, divorce, or other changes. Rituals help us to acknowledge the reality of sadness and disappointments. Friends and relatives can support you in these changes, just as you can reach out and support them. Some of these transitions and mileposts occur every year, such as birthdays and anniversaries. Others are once in a lifetime, such as a wedding or a funeral.

Anniversary events that are important for us to celebrate are _____.

Religion is related to our celebrations because _____.

Some of the ways I enjoy celebrating are _____.

Holidays such as Christmas are fun to share with _____.

A special celebration I appreciated was _____.

Whether formal or informal, celebrations include a joyous perspective that places loss and sadness in the context of the joy of God's love for us.

Ways I celebrate sad or loss events: _____.

FRIENDS

Friendships greatly enrich partners as individuals and as a couple. Each person's friends provide more opportunities for growth and enjoyment of life. These experiences can become part of the couple's conversation. Friendships that are common to both partners can also help partners to gain needed emotional support so that emotional demands are not placed exclusively upon one partner.

> **P**
> **L O V E**
> **W**
> **E**
> **R**
>
> *For I am persuaded that neither death nor life, nor angels nor principalities nor powers, nor things present nor things to come, nor height nor depth, nor any other created thing, shall be able to separate us from the love of God which is in Christ Jesus our Lord (Rom. 8:38–39).*

Friendship is a gift of _____.

Friends who have meant most to me are _____.

What I like best about these friends is _____.

My spouse and I have these friends in common: _____.

My partner does not know these friends: _____.

Times I would prefer to be with my
friend(s) rather than my spouse are _____.

This might be a threat to our marriage in several ways: _____.

This helps our marriage in several ways: _____.

Most couples have private matters that they never discuss with anyone else. Sometimes, however, a friend's viewpoint can help you cope better with a difficulty or find a solution to a problem. You and your spouse should agree about which topics might be shared with others.

Our agreement concerning discussing
private matters with others is _____.

Discuss how friendships can enhance and support your marriage. Consider also how you and your spouse may be able to enhance and encourage your friends in their relationships, such as marriage, career, or other situations.

Some ways we help or encourage our friends are _____.

RELATIVES

Each partner brings family background and experiences into the marriage in many ways. Parents, siblings, and other relatives are present in your mind since you are influenced by what you learned from each of them. Although absent or deceased, these persons still influence you and your partner through the attitudes and response patterns you developed out of your relationships with them.

Some relatives may be more like friends to you, and you do things together because you enjoy each other. To the extent that relatives and in-laws are friends, the comments you considered in the friendship section above also apply.

Relatives who are more like friends are _____.

Relatives become more troublesome to a couple when there are power struggles or unresolved conflicts or value differences between the couple and the other relatives.

We face these unresolved issues
with my relatives: _____.

We face these unresolved issues
with my spouse's relatives: _____.

<table>
<tr><td>**P**
L O V E
W
E
R</td><td>*Because of the hardness of your heart [Moses allowed divorce]. . . . But from the beginning of the creation, God "made them male and female." "For this reason a man shall leave his father and mother and be joined to his wife, and the two shall become one flesh." . . . Therefore what God has joined together, let no one separate (based on Mark 10:5–9).*</td></tr>
</table>

The key decision you and your spouse must make is whether maintaining your marriage is more important than doing what your relatives or in-laws suggest, ask, or pressure you to do. When you and your spouse are able to talk about any relatives, you have power to set appropriate boundaries with them.

How do your expectations about relatives
compare to those of your spouse?_____

Consider the relatives who are closer to you and/or your spouse. What are the positive qualities? What are the annoying characteristics?

Wife's Relatives	*Positive Qualities*	*Problem Qualities*
Father	_____	_____
Mother	_____	_____
Sister(s)	_____	_____
Brother(s)	_____	_____

Wife's Relatives	Positive Qualities	Problem Qualities
Grandparents	_____	_____
Other relatives	_____	_____
Husband's Relatives	*Positive Qualities*	*Problem Qualities*
Father	_____	_____
Mother	_____	_____
Sister(s)	_____	_____
Brother(s)	_____	_____
Grandparents	_____	_____
Other relatives	_____	_____

What special problems do you face in relating to certain relatives? How will you cope with them? _____

_____

What special appreciation can you give or do you give to relatives and friends for the positive supports and encouragements they give to you and/or your spouse?

My relatives have especially helped us by _____.

My spouse's relatives have especially helped us by _____.

Some ways friends have helped us are _____.

Some ways we have helped others are _____.

Chapter 16

Making Good Out of Bad

The tornado flattened the house, leaving debris scattered everywhere. Somehow Luke and Meg were blown out into their yard, but they miraculously escaped harm.

As she surveyed the damage, Meg's fearful face slowly turned into a smile, which grew into laughter and rejoicing.

"What's wrong with you?" Luke questioned. "How can you laugh when everything we own has just been destroyed?"

Between laughs Meg replied, "Luke, we've been married fourteen years, and this is the first time we've been out together since our wedding!"

An optimist sees the gas tank as half full, but a pessimist sees the same reading as half empty. A pessimist sees only lemons, while an optimist makes lemonade out of the lemons. A pessimist says everything is too little and too late, but an optimist describes how to accomplish goals with what is available.

I am optimistic when _____.

I am pessimistic when _____.

My spouse thinks I am _____.

I think my spouse is _____.

CRISES

How do you react when things do not go as you planned or expected? Depending on the extent and severity of the consequences, a crisis occurs when you feel out of control and therefore threatened with some type of harm, either physical or psychological. Situations become crises according to whether you feel that events are happening faster than you can cope with them.

Consider especially your response to crisis events you have faced. You probably could not control whether the events happened. However, you can *always* control your interpretations and reactions to the events. You choose to respond in a particular way to the event, which in itself influences whether it is a major crisis for you and/or your partner and/or others.

A time when I felt out of control and in crisis was _____.

What caused the crisis was _____.

The crisis might have been avoided or reduced by _____.

I was out of control in this situation in these ways: _____.

I felt _____.

To cope, I did _____.

A new skill I developed to resolve the crisis was _____.

Persons who helped me cope with the crisis were _____.

Sometimes a crisis occurs because you need to make a quick decision between two or more desirable outcomes. For example, you may have two very desirable job offers, and the crisis occurs in trying to decide between them, since you cannot accept both offers. Another possibility may be that you enjoy your present job, but your spouse has a once-in-a-lifetime job offer in another part of the world.

A crisis that resulted from my being required
to choose between two desirable outcomes was _____.

I handled it by _____.

I can provide effective help to
my spouse or others in a crisis by _____.

When have you done this? _____

> **P**
> **L O V E**
> **O**
> **W**
> **E**
> **R**
>
> *It is not the events themselves that become crises, but the meanings that each spouse attaches to the events that turn them into crises.*

DISABILITIES AND CHRONIC CONDITIONS

There are times of extraordinary stress and strain when the course of events seems beyond your understanding and control. You may feel unable to cope with the outcomes, especially when you compare an unwanted permanent or long-term (chronic) condition to what you want or expect.

Some disabilities may be easily noticed by you and others, such as paralysis of an arm or leg. Other disabilities may be less obvious, such as a heart condition, diminished eyesight or hearing, or a brain injury.

The usual sequence of reactions to losing an ability is similar to reactions to other losses in life. These reactions may occur in the following order, or they may occur in various combinations at the same time. Often reactions are in layers; you may think you have worked through one type of reaction only to discover later that it recurs in a different form.

A disability (loss of ability) or chronic
condition that I must face is _____.

Shock and surprise are the usual first reactions to a change in abilities. You may respond with disbelief or a feeling that "this can't be happening." Shock helps to numb a person to the initial pain from the change in ability.

In this situation I felt shock in these ways: _____.

I was surprised because _____.

Anger and frustration often emerge out of shock as a mobilization of your resources to attack and defend against the damages and potential threats that your ability loss brings to you as a person. Anger arises out of hurt and pain.

In this situation I felt anger in these ways: _____.

I used this anger to _____.

Denial and bargaining refer to the refusal to acknowledge the loss or change, resulting in futile attempts to put the situation back as it was before the loss. Bargaining usually involves trying to make a deal with God, relatives, or others to try to put things back as they were. Bargaining may take other forms, also, such as believing there is some magic word or treatment that will restore the lost abilities.

In this situation I tried to deny the realities by _____.

Bargains I tried to make were _____.

When things did not change as I wanted, I _____.

Depression usually sets in when your initial anger and bargaining efforts fail to change the disability back into what you had or wanted. Depression takes you out of the loss or danger by closing down your awareness of alternatives and inhibiting your ability to act. You may constantly feel fatigued, unable to eat or sleep, and lose all interest in your spouse, relatives, or friends. Sometimes depression produces its apparent opposite, a very active flurry of activities that keep a person from being aware of the original pain.

In this situation my depression showed up as _____.

I felt things could not be any worse when _____.

Among my feelings were _____.

Readjustment and renewal are also part of the process. At some point in the cycle of denial and depression, you probably said, or thought, that you would acknowledge the loss. That was when readjustment began. You discovered that depression and denial brought pain. The reactive pain can be greater than the original loss because it robs you of your future, your positives, and your resources.

Readjustment means you decide to make the best of a bad situation. You can then begin to consult others who may have faced a similar loss and learn what they did that worked or did not work.

You know readjustment is helping you when you can begin to accept the support of your spouse, friends, relatives, and others who still see you as a valuable person.

Friends, relatives, and other support persons try to understand and comfort you because they care about you. In times when their well-meant efforts don't help much, their warm support and continuing concern for you tell you that you are wanted and needed. Valuing the intent of the giver is another sign of your renewal.

In this situation I decided to admit my loss when _____.

Some ways I started to readjust were _____.

Persons who valued and encouraged me were _____.

Ways this continues today are _____.

MAKING GOOD OUT OF BAD 119

This process of shock, anger, denial, depression, and readjustment usually takes weeks or months. Several of these stages may occur at the same time. You may think you have moved beyond all your anger and are readjusting when something happens to remind you of another part of the loss and your reactions to it. This erratic backward-and-forward pattern is also typical.

Just as others reached out to you in your time of loss, you can remember that when it is your time to be understanding with your spouse or others. Because of your experience, you are able to assist them as others assisted you.

My spouse felt a loss and I was supportive when _____.

> **P**
> **L O V E**
> **W**
> **E**
> **R**
>
> *Comfort each other and edify one another. . . . Always pursue what is good both for yourselves and for all (1 Thess. 5:11, 15).*

FORGIVENESS

When bad things happen to you or other good people, it is easy to assume that life or God or others are unfair and hostile to you. Perhaps the last thing you want to do is to forgive them. However, forgiveness is the breakthrough response that releases your energy for more constructive responses.

Forgiveness means you pardon the offending person or event. You release yourself from having to look for ways to get even. You open yourself to new learning even from a bad situation. Forgiveness is your emotional "reset" button that allows you to restore your life operation to normal (or as near normal as possible).

It is easy to forgive because _____.

It is most difficult to forgive because _____.

I hope I am forgiven by _____.

As Christians, we know that God forgives us. His forgiveness provides the standard for our forgiveness to others.

Forgiveness frees you and the other persons involved. Because of forgiveness, you are free to go on with your lives.

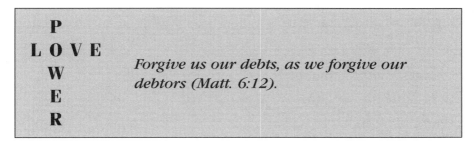

P
L O V E
W   *Forgive us our debts, as we forgive our*
E   *debtors (Matt. 6:12).*
R

LONGER RANGE PLANNING

Longer range planning gives you and your partner the opportunity to create the "for better" side of your relationship. Your goals, intentions, wants, and commitments can be used to shape your future together. This perspective then helps you in both daily tasks and crises.

Through longer range perspectives and planning, you and your spouse can see downtimes as bumps along your journey. When one road is closed, you can choose alternate paths or even alternate goals.

In the longer range view, downtimes can be variations in an otherwise overall satisfactory and happy direction because you work to change the situation.

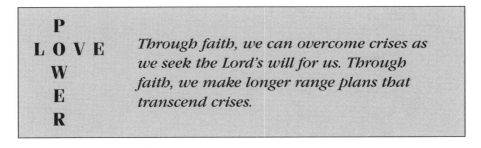

P
L O V E   *Through faith, we can overcome crises as*
W   *we seek the Lord's will for us. Through*
E   *faith, we make longer range plans that*
R   *transcend crises.*

WAYS TO INCREASE THE POSITIVES

In Part 3, we've discussed each of the following elements. Take some time to jot down additional ideas or reminders to yourself about ways to increase your positives. You may want to discuss them with your spouse at this time.

Affection and the sexual relationship: _____.

Money and financial issues: _____.

Lifestyle patterns: _____.

Health and well-being: _____.

Leisure, intimacy, and fun times: _____.

Celebrations, friends, and relatives: _____.

Making good out of bad: _____.

Part 4

EVALUATING YOUR RESOURCES

Managing your abilities and strengths

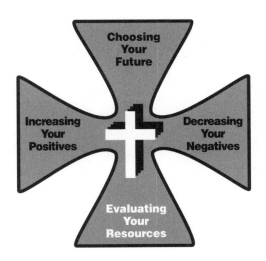

By examining these areas carefully, you can celebrate your strengths and decide how to improve on your resources to share love with your spouse. On this basis each of you can reach out in love to others.

Chapter 17

Genetic Givens

"Hey, shorty!"

"You're so tall. Where did you play basketball?"

"Nearly everyone in my family has died from . . ."

"It just runs in our family."

"Noise never bothers me. I can sleep right through anything."

"How wonderful to have perfect pitch."

"You are too old."

"You are too young."

Comments like these focus on or draw attention to some aspect of a person's physical appearance or physiological system.

Which of these comments fits you? _____

List one or two other comments about your
appearance or abilities that you often receive: _____.

How do you feel about these comments? _____

P
L O V E
W
E
R

Do not worry about your life, what you will eat; nor about the body, what you will put on. . . . And which of you by worrying can add one cubit to his stature? (Luke 12:22, 25).

Your constitution is your physical makeup resulting from your inherited qualities that are modified by your environment. Your physical constitution includes qualities that you and others can see plus many additional factors that are less obvious and indirectly observable. Personality is your characteristic way of behaving.

PHYSICAL APPEARANCE

Appearance includes your height, weight, shape of your face, hair (or lack of it!), skin color and texture, bone structure, age, and other elements that contribute to the way you look. Like it or not, your appearance has a great impact on your spouse and on others. They respond to you as they see you as well as to what you do or do not do. You respond to your partner partly on the basis of appearance.

How do these sayings relate to you and your spouse?

"You can't judge a book by its cover": _____.

"You never have a second chance
to make a good first impression": _____.

"Dress to win": _____.

Some appearance factors are more noticeable in contrast to your spouse. For example, society usually assumes that the husband will be taller than his wife. A wife who is taller than her husband may experience an insensitive person's comments about the difference.

Ways that height, weight, or age
comparisons affect us as a couple are _____.

Other appearance differences include _____.

My reactions to these differences are _____.

My spouse's reactions to these differences are _____.

PHYSIOLOGICAL SENSITIVITY

You and your spouse have certain sensitivity levels for all of your senses. A level of sound may be too loud for one of you, yet too soft for the other. You and your spouse may be comfortable at different room temperatures. In addition, comfort levels may be different while asleep.

How do you use these physiological resources in your marriage?

Sensitivities that we like and use well: _____.

Sensitivities that produce troubling differences: _____.

How we manage these differences: _____.

LIFESTYLE INFLUENCES

Some constitutional factors contribute directly to your lifestyle. For instance, some persons require less sleep than others to maintain good health and vigor. Some persons are more alert and alive earlier in the day, while others are late night persons who are just becoming alive when others are ready for sleep. Lack of sleep may make you tense, irritable, and fatigued. Too much sleep may make you lethargic or may be a sign of depression.

During a twenty-four-hour cycle, at which
times are you most alert and alive? _____

At which times is it most difficult for you to be alert? _____

How do you and your spouse differ in these areas? _____

Your lifestyle pertaining to mealtimes is partly affected by whether you gain or lose weight easily, which in turn affects the types and amounts of food you can eat. If one of you is trying to maintain or lose weight but weight is no problem for the other spouse, how do you handle this in your diet, food menus, and eating out?

My attitudes and feelings about weight and diet are _____.

My spouse's attitudes and feelings about weight and diet are _____.

How do you respect and manage
similarities and differences in these areas? _____

TALENTS AND ABILITIES

In ways that are not well understood, talents such as music and artistic potential are in part inherited. For example, finger dexterity, response speed, rapidity of movement, sound discrimination, and abstract imagery depend upon a person's neuropsychological system. One person may have perfect pitch while another seems to be unable to carry a tune in a sack. These types of potential, of course, may be enhanced or ignored by family, teachers, and friends.

Other intellectual abilities, such as verbal skills, mathematical ability, and sensitivity to emotional reactions, differ among persons and often between spouses. If one spouse is more gifted in a given area than the other, each spouse will need to learn to appreciate personal gifts and possible lack of gifts.

My gifts or talents: _____.

My spouse's gifts or talents: _____.

How we encourage each other: _____.

ACTIVITY LEVELS

You may have a higher or lower activity level than your spouse. The match between the activity levels is important, yet even more important is what both make out of these differences. You choose whether you will be comfortable with these differences, making adjustments and compromises as needed, or whether you will complain about them.

Our attitudes toward differences
in our activity levels are _____.

> P
> L O V E
> W
> E
> R
>
> *Having then gifts differing according to the grace that is given to us, let us use them (Rom. 12:6).*

PERSONAL DIMENSIONS

Here are several dimensions that describe personal characteristics. You can rate yourself on them and then discuss them with your spouse. You will gain more from this activity if you make a copy of this page and ask your spouse to rate you independently. Document clearly the reasons that you describe yourself or your partner in a particular way.

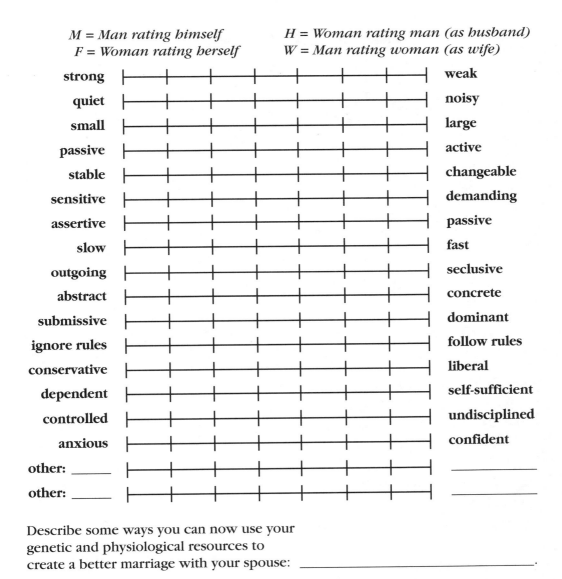

M = Man rating himself   H = Woman rating man (as husband)
F = Woman rating herself   W = Man rating woman (as wife)

strong	weak
quiet	noisy
small	large
passive	active
stable	changeable
sensitive	demanding
assertive	passive
slow	fast
outgoing	seclusive
abstract	concrete
submissive	dominant
ignore rules	follow rules
conservative	liberal
dependent	self-sufficient
controlled	undisciplined
anxious	confident
other: _____	_____
other: _____	_____

Describe some ways you can now use your
genetic and physiological resources to
create a better marriage with your spouse: _____.

Chapter 18

Personality Patterns

"You have the cutest personality," Jack whispered to Jill.

"Is that an insult or a compliment?" Jill smiled back.

"I like the way you do things," Jack continued. "Let's get a pail and go after some water together."

"Sounds like fun. Just be sure we don't trip over our personalities," Jill called as they headed up the hill.

Personality is your characteristic way of behaving. Personality is both who you are and how you act. You might think of your character as your more permanent, inner core self (or "ego" or "I"), and your personality as the sets of patterns that you typically use in relating to your spouse and others.

Out of your genetic givens, temperament, and family experiences across your childhood, adolescence, and adulthood until now, you have formed the patterns that make up your personality. Since you learned them, you can also change them, especially if you and your spouse mutually decide to do so.

On your marriage journey, your personality patterns can either trip up you and your partner or provide refreshing renewal.

There are many dimensions of personality, with many mixtures and shadings.

> **P**
> **L O V E**
> **O**
> **W**
> **E**
> **R**
>
> *Don't let the world squeeze you into its own mold, but be transformed by the renewing of your mind and spirit so you can know the will of God and learn the best possible ways to live (based on Rom. 12:2).*

130 EVALUATING YOUR RESOURCES

SEXUAL IDENTITY AND MARRIAGE

Sexual identity is a major aspect of your personality. Gender usually means only that you have the anatomical characteristics of a male or female human being. Sexual identity refers to your interpretations of what it means to have male or female physical characteristics. You express your personality through all the sexual activities you and your spouse have. To emphasize the unity of personality and sexuality, many experts point to your brain as your most important sex organ.

Can you remember when you first
discovered you were a girl or boy? _____

How do you feel about being your gender? _____

Have you ever wished you could enjoy
the advantages of being the other sex? _____

My advantage or disadvantage in
being the sex that I am is _____.

I have these healthy attitudes about
myself and about members of the other sex: _____.

Some hurtful attitudes I have about
myself and about members of the other sex are _____.

I plan to change these hurtful
opinions into more helpful attitudes by _____.

ASSUMPTIONS AND EXPECTATIONS

Many assumptions and expectations about your marriage come from your observations of your parents, your grandparents, and other couples in your extended family. You may anticipate that your spouse will usually act like your parent of the other sex. This implies that you will probably act like your same-sex parent, unless you are aware of this possibility.

My reactions to my parents' marriage(s) are _____.

Ways I will vary my reactions so that my spouse and I have freedom to create our own marriage are _____.

The same effects hold for your spouse.

For the husband: My wife is likely to respond to me as she saw her mother as a wife respond to her husband. My wife is probably going to assume that I will respond to her as she observed her father treat her mother in their marriage.

The characteristics were _____.

I am likely to respond to my wife as I saw my father (as a husband) respond to my mother (as his wife). I am also likely to anticipate that my wife will respond to me as I observed my mother respond to my father in their marriage.

The characteristics were _____.

For the wife: My husband is likely to respond to me as he saw his father as a husband respond to his mother. My husband is probably going to assume that I will respond to him as he observed his mother treat his father in their marriage.

The characteristics were _____.

I am likely to respond to my husband as I saw my mother (as a wife) respond to my father (as her husband). I am also likely to anticipate that my husband will respond to me as I observed my father respond to my mother in their marriage.

The characteristics were _____.

If your family of origin was broken by death, desertion, or divorce, you may have additional stepparents whose influences are added to these dynamics.

Some of these influences include _____.

If I react to my parents in these ways, my parents probably reacted to their parents (my grandparents) in similar ways, also.

PERSONAL HABITS

Here are some habits that are sometimes troublesome for a couple. Some are individual, and some involve both partners. All, however, affect the spouse as well as the person with the habit.

Consider each item and decide whether it is a problem in your marriage. Each partner can mark the chart independently, and then you can compare your answers and discuss them. Note that your answers refer to habits of your spouse.

My Spouse's Habit	Does Not Do This; Okay as Is	This Habit Bothers Me			
		Very Much	Some	Very Little	Not at All
Being late for appointments	_____	_____	_____	_____	_____
Dressing inappropriately	_____	_____	_____	_____	_____
Keeping an untidy house	_____	_____	_____	_____	_____
Using tobacco	_____	_____	_____	_____	_____
Using alcoholic beverages	_____	_____	_____	_____	_____
Using illegal drugs	_____	_____	_____	_____	_____
Driving too fast or carelessly	_____	_____	_____	_____	_____
Using slang or profanity	_____	_____	_____	_____	_____
Ignoring me; leaving me out	_____	_____	_____	_____	_____
Nagging; putting me down	_____	_____	_____	_____	_____
Being overly critical	_____	_____	_____	_____	_____
Squeezing toothpaste tube from the middle	_____	_____	_____	_____	_____
Other: _____	_____	_____	_____	_____	_____

If you feel tense discussing these more troublesome habits, take a break and express your appreciation to each other. It will also help to provide specific examples that you can use to modify the habit and agree on which changes each of you will make.

Here are some desirable, positive habits and behaviors. Again, independently check them as they refer to your spouse. After you complete the list, discuss examples of each.

My Spouse's Habit, Behavior, or Characteristic	Does Not Do This; Okay as Is	Please Do This			
		Much More	More	Same	Less
Being on time for appointments	_____	_____	_____	_____	_____
Encouraging me	_____	_____	_____	_____	_____

My Spouse's Habit, Behavior, or Characteristic	Does Not Do This; Okay as Is	Please Do This		
		Much More	More	Same	Less
Grooming for an attractive appearance	_____	_____	_____	_____	_____
Being considerate	_____	_____	_____	_____	_____
Being honest and truthful	_____	_____	_____	_____	_____
Being thoughtful	_____	_____	_____	_____	_____
Having a sense of humor	_____	_____	_____	_____	_____
Expressing affection	_____	_____	_____	_____	_____
Willing to be open and flexible	_____	_____	_____	_____	_____
Being cooperative; working together	_____	_____	_____	_____	_____
Showing respect for others and for me	_____	_____	_____	_____	_____
Taking care of property	_____	_____	_____	_____	_____
Other: _____	_____	_____	_____	_____	_____

HOW I FEEL ABOUT MYSELF

For each item, circle a number to show where you are.

	Strongly Disagree	Dis-agree	Maybe	Agree	Strongly Agree
1. I can usually accomplish goals that I set for myself.	1	2	3	4	5
2. If others knew me better, they would probably choose someone else.	1	2	3	4	5

	Strongly Disagree	Dis-agree	Maybe	Agree	Strongly Agree
3. I can wait patiently for good things to happen because they usually do.	1	2	3	4	5
4. I try to please others rather than do what I really would enjoy.	1	2	3	4	5
5. I make better decisions when I take time to check out all the angles.	1	2	3	4	5
6. I find it embarrassing and confusing to ask anyone for help or directions.	1	2	3	4	5
7. Accepting reality gives me confidence to find solutions to problems.	1	2	3	4	5
8. It is better to pretend that things are okay than to be disappointed by facts.	1	2	3	4	5
9. Most people think I can do well in marriage and in life.	1	2	3	4	5
10. I prefer to accept the first offer rather than risk not getting anything better.	1	2	3	4	5

Key for How I Feel About Myself

First, add the numbers you circled for statements 1, 3, 5, 7, and 9.   = _____
Next, add the numbers you circled for statements 2, 4, 6, 8, and 10, and then subtract this total from 30.   = _____
Add these two totals to get your self-esteem estimate.   Total: _____
Your score can be between 10 and 50.

The higher your score, the more likely that you have higher self-esteem and more self-confidence. Higher self-esteem gives you a more solid foundation for making decisions and greater stability. Higher self-esteem often comes out of having experienced healthy ways of living. This confidence enables you to hold to what is good, yet be open to changes.

Don't get hung up in comparing numbers with your spouse, however. An overemphasis on numbers and comparisons can also be a sign of lower self-esteem. Instead, you will learn more about yourself if you review each statement and modify it to express the real you. After your spouse also does this, you can talk about what you like about your personality and what you want to change.

> **P**
> **L O V E**
> **W**
> **E**
> **R**
>
> *Present yourselves to God as being alive from the dead, and your members as instruments of righteousness to God (Rom. 6:13).*

Chapter 19

Families of Origin

"Our family was really fun. Mom, Dad, and all the kids were nearly always together for the evening meal. We would talk about anything, disagree, and laugh. Either Dad or Mom would ask us how things were going, and we would cheer about our wins and cry when things went wrong. We were really for each other. It was great."

"Mom was sick a long time before she died. Dad helped us adjust as best he could, but we all missed her. About three years later he married a woman who also had children. As they say, we just blended together. There were some conflicts, but generally, we worked things out together."

"When my mother and father split up, neither one wanted us. We were passed from one foster home to another. Finally, a church children's home took us in. We lived in family style cottages with houseparents. While I was there, we had three different sets of houseparents. It could have been better, but it could have been a lot worse."

How would you describe your childhood family? Try writing a brief description of what it was like for you in your family.

_____

_____

_____

You learned the basics of who you are in your childhood and adolescence as part of your family of origin. Family of origin is the group of persons who lived with you in your home, whether related by blood ties, marriage, legal decisions, friendship, or other circumstances. In your family of origin you learned many of the rules, assumptions, styles, skills, values, and other characteristics that you hold important or reject today.

In families, adults control the quality of the household for the persons who live in it. For this reason, this workbook focuses on you and your spouse as a couple. You are the adults who control what happens in your household.

Who had most control in your childhood family? _____

Who had least control? _____

How did you feel about this power distribution? _____

You and your spouse are invited to look at your families of origin in four different ways. (You may want to save this information since you may want to pass it along to your children someday.)

Through these perspectives, you can see how each of you developed the personality patterns, skills, and habits you bring to your marriage. By knowing your history, you can free yourself to see strengths and weaknesses from your past. Then you can evaluate your resources so you can modify and improve them in your current relationship as spouses and with others.

1. YOUR FAMILY STRUCTURE: THE CAST OF CHARACTERS

Identify the persons you consider as your family of origin.

The adults in your family: _____.

Birth order and sex of children: _____.

Others in your childhood home: _____.

Changes in family structure across your childhood
years (for example, deaths, divorces, remarriages): _____.

Write the names of your parents, brothers, sisters, other relatives, and very close friends. Then use a word or phrase to describe the best quality about each person. Try to identify the unique contribution that each person has given you.

_____

_____

Now, consider the males and females separately. How are the men in your family alike and different?

Some positive qualities
of the men in my family are _____.

Some negative characteristics
of the men in my family are _____.

How are the women in your family alike and different?

Some positive qualities
of the women in my family are _____.

Some negative characteristics
of the women in my family are _____.

Each person in your family has (or had) a place with both privileges and limitations in relation to other family members. Power balances in your family (who is in control or not) were set in relation to family members' needs and goals. These power balances shifted as you grew older and other persons entered or left your home setting.

What patterns of power balances do
you see in your family of origin? _____

How did being male or female, older or
younger, influence who had power in your family? _____

How do these assumptions about roles and
power affect you now in your marriage? _____

2. YOUR FAMILY TIME LINE HISTORY

Another way to picture your family is with a time line. To do this, each partner will need a very large sheet of paper, such as newsprint or plain wrapping paper. If that is not available, piece together several sheets of paper. Mark one large sheet with the wife's name and the other with the husband's name.

At the bottom of each large sheet, draw a horizontal line with short marks to divide the line into years from your parents' marriage until your marriage. Number the short marks beginning with the year of your parents' marriage. Enter their names. Above your birth year, place your name, and add names and other details of your sisters, brothers, and others in your family.

On each sheet for each year, place names, words, and phrases to note important events in your family, along with the impact each event had on you.

As you and your spouse discuss your time lines, note how your memory of family events may make you more or less confident as you enter the same age a parent or other family member was when something especially good or bad happened. By tracing your unconscious associations to ages or relationships in your past, you become more aware of how your family background continues to influence you. You will be free to increase your power to love your spouse now.

Look at your family history and compare it with your partner's family history. In this way you can uncover sources of hurt and pain, hidden reasons that certain events trigger strong emotions in you, and causes for celebrating your unique possibilities.

3. YOUR FAMILY TREE

Your family tree gives you the roots for your marriage. To see your roots as a couple, each spouse will need another sheet of paper large enough to place the names of all of the persons in the family tree.

> **P**
> **L O V E**
> **W**
> **E**
> **R**
>
> *I call to remembrance the genuine faith that is in you, which dwelt first in your grandmother Lois and your mother Eunice, and I am persuaded is in you also. Therefore I remind you to stir up the gift of God which is in you through the laying on of my hands. For God has not given us a spirit of fear, but of power and of love and of a sound mind (2 Tim. 1:5–7).*

For a very simple family tree, let circles stand for females, squares for males. For each generation, place a symbol to represent each person in that generation on the same horizontal line. By each name, place birth and death dates. Add dates for marriages and divorces. Connect the symbols for your parents as husband and wife, then add any stepparents, or other parenting persons in your family.

Begin your family tree with your generation, showing your siblings on the same line as yours but in slightly smaller size. Indicate your family by drawing vertical lines to a horizontal generational line. Continue this process for your parents' generation, and then to your grandparents. Go to previous generations if you can. If you have children, place them on the next horizontal line below yours.

History is "event plus interpretation." Your family history contains many interrelated events to which you and others attached interpretations. As you describe your family tree, add notes about the interpretations you give to the persons and situations you review.

These interpretations may be positive (*for example, birth of child*) or negative (*for example, death of sibling or parent*).

A positive event I desire is _____.

A negative event I fear is _____.

Events may be serious (*for example, threat of nuclear war*) or mild (*for example, child starts to nursery school*).

For me, a serious event is _____.

A mild event is _____.

Family Life Cycle Fit

Did the major life events occur at typical or usual times for your family? If so, you probably adjusted to them as a normal part of life. If not, you may have felt hurt or cheated. Either way, your experience may lead you to expect or anticipate similar sequences in your marital journey.

Who moved out of your family early
(before age nineteen or so)? Why? _____

Who is still at home with one
or both parents? Why? _____

Other transitions, such as completing education,
career changes, and change of residence, include _____.

A recent family conflict or issue is _____.

A past event that still bothers me is _____.

Repeated Patterns Across Generations

What patterns, either good or bad, appear in successive generations of your family?

Alcoholism, other drug abuse: _____.

Physical illnesses, violence, suicide: _____.

Job loss, poverty: _____.

Physical disabilities: _____.

Divorce, desertion: _____.

Career successes: _____.

Patterns of sudden events: _____.

Gradual or long-standing disease: _____.

Life Events and Family Functioning

There may be connections between events in your family. For example, a child may marry only after the death of a parent or marry as a reaction to a loss of some kind.

Which events seem to be connected in your family? _____

Did you lose one or both parents through separation, divorce, or death? If so, what remarriages brought different adults into your life?

Marriage changes in my parents' lives: _____.

How I felt (and feel) about these changes: _____.

How I have coped with this: _____.

Social, economic, and political events in the community or society, such as a family member being called to wartime service, may have had major impacts on your family.

Which outside events were especially important for your family? _____

Patterns for Power

In your family you may have learned that certain family members always agreed or fought over any issue. These expressed power alignments or struggles that continue to affect you now.

Was your family enmeshed, close, distant, or chaotic? _____

Who controlled what you and other family members did? _____

What patterns of power do you
see in your family of origin? _____

Family Values and Rules

Every family has a set of values and goals, both openly stated and assumed. The resources of the family are allocated to achieve these goals. What are some key values your family held? What values did your parents have in common?

_____

_____

Problem Solving

Your parents and other family members had conflicts and disagreements. They may have resolved them in private, discussed them calmly with all the family, or argued endlessly with no good solutions.

The usual way my parents resolved disagreements was _____.

What impressions of marriage did you gain
from the way your parents solved problems? _____

Rules About Making Rules

Metarules are rules about making rules. For example, in a sports contest, the teams agree on the boundaries and other rules by which they play. There are usually rules about how to make the rules, like parliamentary procedures. These metarules guide decisions about the playing rules.

Your family had rules about how and when a rule was changed. For example, a parent might say, "I'm the parent. I can change the rule if I want." A better metarule is that every person who is affected by a rule must be included in making or changing a rule.

Guidelines we have about making rules for our marriage: _____.

4. FAMILY MEMBERS WHO INFLUENCED YOU

Think of the persons who have shaped your life. What has each taught you? What dreams have they encouraged you to have? Think of the special persons in your life in each of these categories. Describe how you feel about these persons.

Relationship with my mother: _____.

Lessons she taught me: _____.

Dreams she encouraged: _____.

Ideals or goals she helped me to form: _____.

Relationship with my father: _____.

Lessons he taught me: _____.

Dreams he encouraged: _____.

Ideals or goals he helped me to form: _____.

Relationships with grandparents: _____.

Lessons they taught me: _____.

Dreams they encouraged: _____.

Ideals or goals they helped me to form: _____.

Other relatives (first names): _____.

Lessons they taught me: _____.

Dreams they encouraged: _____.

Ideals or goals they helped me to form: _____.

My best role model: _____.

My best reward: _____.

Ways I am a good role model: _____.

YOUR PERSONAL HISTORY TIME LINE

List key happenings in your life and describe the effects on you. Add names of the key persons in these events. Place year date in the left column.

Age/Year	*Event*	*Effect/Impact on Me*

0–5 (Early Childhood):

6–11 (Elementary School):

12–17 (Junior High/High School):

18–early 20s:

Late 20s–30s:

Late 30s–40s:

50s and later:

EXITING YOUR FAMILY OF ORIGIN

As you and your spouse review your family backgrounds, you probably will see some qualities and patterns that you like and want to continue. You will also see other patterns that you want to modify or perhaps eliminate. Love power is the standard by which you decide how to use your previous family experiences in your marriage. From Old Testament times, the important wisdom of a man leaving his parents and cleaving (or bonding) to his wife has been a fundamental emphasis of marriage. Since men and women are coequal before God, this advice applies equally to a woman leaving her parents and bonding with her husband to form a new family unit ("body" or "flesh").

Patterns I learned in my family of origin
that I want to continue in my marriage: _____.

Patterns from my family of origin that
I want to change in my marriage: _____.

Leaving your childhood family means that you move from being a child of your parents to being an adult in relation to them as adults. In a sense you separate from your parents to discover a deeper relationship as friends in Christ.

YOUR CHOICES ABOUT YOUR MARRIAGE

Marriage requires that you renegotiate all of your earlier patterns with another person (your spouse) whose past history is similar and dissimilar in many ways, and that you live with the results in your marriage.

In a healthy family, a person learns to make choices about skills and goals. You appreciate those who helped you, and as an independent adult, you cooperate to reach common goals. In an unhealthy family, parents and others try to tie children to themselves and keep children from making their own choices. This is one major difference between flexibility and enmeshment.

Ways I see love as a choice: _____.

Some sources of my strength to love: _____.

An unhealthy parent may try to relive life through the child's life and activities by pushing the child to do what the parent wants, such as drill team, cheerleading, sports, and other activities. In contrast, a healthy parent encourages imagination in the child, so both parent and child can seek to fulfill dreams in realistic and loving ways.

You express your choices, your personality or personal strategy for living, in the ways you use your skills and resources. Acting on your choices usually takes effort, work, sweat, blood, and tears. These actions strengthen your skills for increasing positive outcomes that reach your goals. These actions also strengthen your skills that keep you on a safe and timely life and marriage journey.

Some good I celebrate: _____.

How my spouse and I can
use this in our marriage now: _____.

> **P**
> **L O V E**
> **W**
> **E**
> **R**
>
> *Every person chooses many times every day—whether to*
> *. . . give a cheery hello or grunt a foul curse.*
> *. . . listen to another's hurt or force pain on another.*
> *. . . be part of the problem or be part of the solution.*
> *. . . change for the better or drift into making it worse.*

Chapter 20

Ethnic, National, and Cultural Factors

"In the old country we never did it this way. I just can't get used to the way the young people live today."

"Sis, when will I ever be old enough to make my own decisions without your comments?" said a very successful man, age seventy-five, to his eighty-one-year-old sister.

"There's a certain way to do a wedding. Your grandparents did it that way. We did it that way. Why do you want to change it?"

"I lived with you in your country for the first twenty years we were married. Why don't you want to move to my country for a few years?"

You and your spouse bring different ways of doing marriage from your families of origin. Additional influences and traditions come from your ethnic, national, socioeconomic, religious, and cultural heritages. How you feel about differences is far more important than whether you have differences.

Important similarities: _____.

Important differences: _____.

How we negotiate them: _____.

Ethnic, racial, or national factors
that are important for our marriage: _____.

How we use them to benefit our marriage: _____.

Factors that cause difficulties for us: _____.

There is neither Jew nor Greek, there is neither slave nor free, there is neither male nor female, for you are all one in Christ Jesus (Gal. 3:28).

When education and socioeconomic status are part of the ethnic equation, even more variations occur. Professional persons from different ethnic and cultural groups may have more in common with each other than with laborers from their own ethnic group.

Educational factors that affect us are _____.

Ways that financial differences
between our families affect us are _____.

Your awareness of and appreciation for your ethnic heritage come through the many developmental experiences outside your family. They come through the encounters with friends, with teachers at school, with community groups, and with other types of authorities in your community. Think of two or three of these experiences that impress you today.

What would you like to change about them? _____

What do you value about them? _____

LEAVING YOUR HERITAGE

To leave your parents as parents opens you to the possibilities of a new adult-to-adult relationship with them (and other family members) as adult friends who share a common heritage and continue to be concerned about each other throughout life. Whether racial, ethnic, international, or cultural, you and your spouse continue to weave the strands of your heritage into your marriage. In this process you take your place within or outside that heritage.

It probably will take twenty or thirty years after reaching adulthood for you to completely leave your parents and fully cleave to your spouse. Whether your parents are alive or dead, their parental models and instructions, along with your attitudes toward them, still influence you in many ways.

Some parental models that still influence me are _____.

My feelings about my heritage are _____.

KEEPING YOUR HERITAGE

Most persons remember the past in the form of stories about specific events or happenings. The way you remember an event may be quite different from the way your parent, brother, sister, or friend remembers that event. Your grandparents' views about your parents also add insights to your heritage. What are some favorite stories you received from other family members?

Grandparents: _____.

Aunts, uncles: _____.

Sisters, brothers: _____.

How my views influence other relatives: _____.

You can also preserve your heritage through family pictures, videotapes, and news articles. You may value items that were used by your parents, grandparents, or others in your family.

DEPENDENCE, INDEPENDENCE, INTERDEPENDENCE, AND COOPERATION

As a healthy individual, you moved from the dependency of infancy to being independent with your own sense of autonomy and confidence. That led to your adult interdependence, which makes possible cooperation with others. The dependency-to-interdependencies dimension appears in every aspect of your marriage.

P
L O V E
W
E
R

To understand your partner, begin by understanding your partner's heritage. To understand yourself, begin by understanding your heritage.

Your ethnic and cultural context may define specific ways you are to relate to your spouse, other family members, your heritage, and your community. Your cultural patterns may express any of these three types of relationships.

Dependence

In what ways do you still depend on your parents? In what ways do they continue to depend on you? Are these ways appropriate?

_____

_____

Independence

As you have become independent from your family of origin, how have they learned to be independent from you? If your parents have an empty nest with all their children away from home, how are they enjoying this stage of their lives? How are you handling your adult complexities of being autonomous?

_____

_____

Interdependence

How do you and your relatives work together for goals you hold in common? Identify the contributions that each participating family member must make to achieve the cooperation that you want. What are your procedures for modifying the agreements, both explicit and implicit, that maintain your systems of cooperation?

_____

_____

YOUR LEARNING STYLE HERITAGE

Out of your unique combination of genetic and environmental factors, you have developed your special learning style. For example, you may pay more attention to what you see than what you hear. You may be able to remember names better than faces. Your spouse also has a special learning style, which may be different from yours.

I am best at learning _____.

I am poorest at learning _____.

The ways I learn least are through _____.

The ways I learn best are through _____.

This learning style affects our marriage by _____.

P
L O V E
W
E
R

Whoever does the will of My Father in heaven is My brother and sister and mother (Matt. 12:50).

A learning style is never right or wrong. It is, however, more or less functional in a given set of circumstances. Becoming aware of the relative strengths and weaknesses of your learning style is an important element in your personal inventory.

Your family and ethnic heritage contributes to your learning style. Before God, all differences are valuable because God loves every person. In the context of God's grace and love, your key is being open to learning how to love in the specific circumstances of your marriage, your community, and our world.

Chapter 21

Networks for Support

*"It takes a lot of effort to get up, get ready, and go to church each week,"
Paul commented as he buttoned his shirt.*

*"Yes, but it's worth it," replied Kay. "I am renewed through worship and
prayer. I also enjoy visiting with our friends and sharing what has been
happening the past week."*

*"So do I," Paul added. "It does get hectic at times, yet it's encouraging to
know that in our community there are others who are committed to God
and want life to be better."*

*"Remember we are hosting our neighborhood watch group next Tuesday,"
Kay reminded as she finished her makeup. "They are counting on you to
have that security information."*

"I have it," confirmed Paul. "How about a security hug for the road?"

You need several personal support networks, just as you are part of the support
networks for others. Among these networks are churches, schools, and other organizations in your community. In addition to your relatives, you have informal
support persons in neighbors and friends with whom you have coffee or exchange visits.

Support networks enable you to multiply the resources that give you power to be
who you are, shape your marriage in the ways you do, and in so many more ways
express the love that you want to give.

My important groups: _____.

How these groups help me: _____.

Ways I help others through these groups: _____.

In addition to family and other relatives, many persons influence and support you and your spouse in your marriage. They strengthen your values, patterns, and skills for living. They encourage your dreams and goals. They model a clear faith in God.

Think of persons who influence you now. What has each taught you? What dreams do they encourage you to have? Think of two or three special persons in your life in each of these categories.

1. Our friends: _____.

   Skills they teach me or us: _____.

   Plans they encourage: _____.

   Suggestions they offer: _____.

2. Our teachers, coaches, leaders: _____.

   Skills they teach me or us: _____.

   Goals they encourage: _____.

3. Other groups and persons: _____.

   Skills they taught or teach us: _____.

   Plans they encourage: _____.

   Perspectives they provide: _____.

> **P**
> **L O V E**
> **W**
> **E**
> **R**
>
> *Fulfill my joy by being like-minded, having the same love, being . . . of one mind. Let nothing be done through selfish ambition or conceit. . . . Let this mind be in you which was also in Christ Jesus (Phil. 2:2-5).*

GROUP SUPPORTS FOR YOUR FAITH EXPRESSIONS

Participating as a couple in your church supports your marriage and your personal faith. Your involvement in other community improvement groups, such as political action, environmental protection, or energy solutions, can also express your personal faith and commitments about life. Participation in these groups involves voluntary time commitments, money, leadership roles, and attendance at meetings.

Groups we enjoy as a couple: _____.

How we can cooperate concerning our
church and other group participation: _____.

How are your personal faith perspectives
related to your religious tradition?_____

Here are some types of group involvements that may express your personal faith. In which do you and your spouse want to be involved as part of your marriage? Discuss your current involvements, if any, in contrast to what you would like to do. Name specific groups, if possible.

Worship services: _____.

Study and fellowship groups in church: _____.

Committees: _____.

Leadership, teaching: _____.

Charitable, religious, or arts causes: _____.

Civic improvement organizations: _____.

Health and welfare organizations: _____.

Political action group or political party: _____.

Other groups: _____.

MOVING AND OTHER SUPPORT NETWORK DISRUPTIONS

Changing your residence greatly affects your support networks.

Think of the changes of residence that you or your family have made.

How often have you moved during your life? _____

How has moving affected you? _____

Do you anticipate moving as a couple? _____

If so, under what circumstances?
How often? For which reasons? _____

If not, what factors will enable
you to remain in the same community? _____

How do you and your spouse feel about these possibilities? _____

Moving involves these factors. Select the ones that are important for you and/or your partner, and discuss how you will cope with each factor: losing friends; finding new friends; packing belongings; losing social groups; locating a desirable residence; becoming part of a new community; changing physician, attorney, church, other professional persons; and adjusting children to a new environment.

COMMITMENTS: CLARIFYING SUPPORT GROUPS

You make commitments to some groups and do not join others because of the values, goals, and persons you find in them. Commitments express your desire to hold to certain values and goals.

How do you relate your commitment to each other as spouses with your commitments and decisions about your support groups and networks?

Ways my support groups express my commitments include _____.

The most important goals in my life are _____.

INTEGRATING YOUR STRENGTHS FOR MARRIAGE

In Part 4, we've discussed each of the following elements. Take some time to jot down additional ideas or reminders to yourself about ways to strengthen your marriage. You may want to discuss them with your spouse at this time.

Constitution and temperament: _____.

Personalities: _____.

Previous family experiences: _____.

Ethnic and other factors: _____.

Support groups and networks: _____.

Part 5

DECREASING YOUR NEGATIVES

Replacing hurtful patterns with healthy skills

Decreasing your negatives refers to hurtful conditions that push spouses apart and destroy their marriage relationship. The goal of these chapters is to enable you and your spouse to decide to reduce or eliminate the negatives in your marriage. Any one of the following conditions will destroy your marriage if you do not do something positive about it.

In each situation both partners must decide to eliminate the negative and then take steps to replace it with more positive patterns. Coping effectively with any of these negative situations will probably require professional help. There are entire books on each of the negatives in this section. (Part 7 provides some guidance about finding appropriate professional treatment.)

If you are not personally involved in any of these detrimental situations, this is a good time to rejoice with your spouse. You can increase your confidence and skills for your marriage by confronting each possible negative in this section and deciding on your love power strategies. When you enhance your positives, you crowd out hurtful patterns. In this way you prevent the negatives from ever happening.

> **P**
> **L O V E**
> **W**
> **E**
> **R**
>
> *We eliminate negatives not by concentrating on them but by replacing them with something better (see Luke 11:24-26; 1 Pet. 3:8-9).*

If you are personally involved in one or more of these negative situations, consider how it is now affecting you, your spouse, and your families. Even if your partner does not want to change, you can make positive changes in yourself. Often your constructive changes will alter the situation so that your partner is encouraged to change in response to your changes, not to your commands or demands for change.

The negatives that now
face us in our marriage are _____.

The strategies we now are
using to cope with them are _____.

I feel this way about the results
of what we are now doing: _____.

You may be stuck in negative patterns because of the influence of others in your lives, such as relatives, neighbors, friends, or persons with whom you work or play. Dealing well with your negatives may also involve confronting your negative influences from other persons.

Chapter 22

Falling Out of Love

A husband and a wife were very angry with each other. As the wife hurried out the back door, she noticed a battered oil lamp. Remembering the story of Aladdin's magic lamp, and with nothing to lose, she decided to rub the lamp, just in case it also was magic. Sure enough, out came a genie! "I will grant you three wishes, but remember that your husband will get twice the amount of whatever you receive."

Not a bad deal at all, she thought. "I would like a million dollars."

"You have it," the genie immediately complied. "And your husband now has two million."

For her second wish the wife, still upset and angry, asked for a fancy new car.

The genie immediately produced a new automobile for the wife. As she climbed into it, the wife caught a glance of the two new automobiles her husband had now acquired.

Even more upset because her husband was getting more than she was, the shrewd woman paused, then uttered her third wish. "Please scare me half to death!"

Hurtful experiences bring by-products of anger, rage, fear, and a desire for revenge and getting even. In the heat of battle the last thing you or your spouse may want to do is to compromise, forgive, and try again to make things work.

Negatives are difficult to read about and even more difficult to discuss with anyone, especially with your partner. However, when any marriage drifts apart or explodes, somewhere there is a series of negative patterns that destroyed the marriage.

FALLING OUT OF LOVE

Falling out of love begins with small things. Spouse A forgets to do something that is important to Spouse B, fails to thank Spouse B for doing something nice, or makes more and more decisions without consulting Spouse B.

Spouse B backs away some, becomes cautious or suspicious, and takes some of the emotional investment out of the marriage. Sensing this slight withdrawal, Spouse A gives Spouse B fewer hugs, spends more time elsewhere, and seems more distant. Spouse B may complain, withdraw, or pursue Spouse A in an effort to bring love back. And so the pattern continues until soon each spouse feels out of love with the other.

Is this pattern happening in your marriage? _____

If so, describe the sequence of
behaviors that you and your spouse
are doing to produce this pattern: _____.

If not, describe how you heal small
hurts before they become big hurts: _____.

SEEING THE SOURCES OF WITHDRAWAL

When one spouse withdraws from the other and from talk, sex, and other activities that formerly were fun times, each responds to some type of hurt or pain. This often is connected to some old images and patterns that you and your spouse brought into your marriage.

Withdrawal reminds me of these painful patterns: _____.

You take your first step toward changing a negative when you become aware of it.

Describe a negative in your
marriage that you want to change: _____.

Next, search for what might have led up to this negative situation.

Some recent changes in our marriage
that might be related to this negative are _____

Some recent events outside our marriage
that might be related to this negative are _____

Recent events may trigger latent or dormant factors in each spouse's background that were earlier repressed, ignored, or overlooked.

Some factors in wife's background that
might be now affecting our marriage are _____.

Some factors in husband's background that
might be now affecting our marriage are _____.

You change because you and your spouse are doing some things differently now as compared to earlier.

Some small things that have become
worse over the past months or years are _____.

Some things I may be doing differently
from what I did earlier in our marriage are _____.

> **P**
> **L O V E**
> **W**
> **E**
> **R**
>
> *Forgiveness frees the one giving it as well as the one receiving it.*

FORGIVING ALL WHO ARE INVOLVED

Your desire to change withdrawal into intimacy begins with forgiveness to all who cause the withdrawal. Through forgiveness, you can make a fresh start toward a new and deeper love for each other.

The good news of the Christian message of love power forgiveness begins with your willingness to confess your part in the hurt and pain. Only after you admit that you might be wrong can you realize and use God's grace and unconditional love. When you say you are well, you shut out God as the Great Physician of love.

God loves you as you are, not as you proclaim yourself to be. It is not a matter of being better or perfect to earn God's love. Since negatives come out of your own fundamental feeling of being unloved, hurt, rejected, or abandoned, only the outreach of God to you can heal the core hurt.

Forgiveness is the way of resetting your relationship, of admitting a mess and starting again with the goal of making things different.

A specific time I admitted to my spouse
that I had made an error or mistake: _____.

How this reset or freed us
to work out a better solution: _____.

If you are not able to get through the forgiveness step, you probably need help from other persons who are not directly involved with your situation, such as a well-trained professional. (See more information in Part 7.)

DECIDING YOU WANT TO CHANGE

The next step after mutual forgiveness is the decision to change. You need to consider your decisions about your future and to reevaluate your resources.

My feelings about rebuilding our marriage intimacy are _____.

The painful pattern I want to change is _____.

The painful pattern my spouse wants to change is _____.

My feelings about being able to do this are _____.

My spouse's feelings about being able to do this are _____.

REBUILDING POSITIVE INTIMACY

Rebuilding positive intimacy is wooing your spouse to a new, fresh, and exciting relationship with you. Intimacy involves finding ways to have fun together and enjoy being with each other as very special friends.

Your differences about intimacy may relate to the different ways that men and women use verbal communication. For instance, talk may be more helpful to a woman, but action may be more helpful to a man. A wife may talk to share views, express feelings, and increase common bonds. In contrast, a husband may talk to get something done.

My feelings about talk in our marriage are _____.

My feelings about silence and action are _____.

Times when talk feels like a command are _____.

Times when silence feels lonely are _____ , _____ .

You can rebuild positive intimacy by putting the love you intend into both talk and actions that your spouse can safely understand as care and warmth.

MAKING TALK SAFE WITH TIME-OUTS

Negatives are difficult to discuss for many reasons. You may be afraid of hurting your spouse or of being hurt. You may think that if you bring up a difficult topic, your spouse will ignore or reject you.

How I feel about discussing negatives: _____ .

How my spouse feels about discussing negatives: _____ .

You can turn to the basic principles of problem solving in Part 6. As you consider these challenging issues, agree to a time-out if you get into an argument.

The time-out technique is comparable to time-outs in sports, allowing the players, coaches, and referees to consult about rule interpretations, to consider information, or to rest a bit before continuing the game. To use the time-out technique, you and your spouse must first agree that taking a time-out is allowed.

Our name for time-out is _____ .

Our time-out signal is _____ .

Length of time-out will usually be _____ .

P
L O V E   *Be kind to one another, tenderhearted,*
W   *forgiving one another, even as God in*
E   *Christ forgave you (Eph. 4:32).*
R

Experiencing withdrawal feels like being on a merry-go-round and repeating the same old patterns but not finding any way to stop them and get off. Your first step is to decide that you want to get off.

A merry-go-round I want to stop is _____.

I most often feel loss in
our marriage relationship when _____.

I want to increase our
intimacy in this area: _____.

To do this, I will try to _____.

Chapter 23

Depression and Other Mental Health Conditions

"I don't know what has come over Bob," Karen commented as she and Marge jogged along their usual trail.

"Oh, Bob's the life of the party," Marge quipped.

"He used to be. Lately he just sits staring into space. He wants to quit work. He won't eat right." Karen paused, then added, "I even put on my sexy nightie, and he just smiled and went off to sleep."

Marge tried to reassure Karen: "Wow! That doesn't sound like Bob. Maybe he will snap out of it."

"But I'm worried that he won't. Do you have any ideas that might help?"

What would you suggest each person could do? _____

If I were in each person's situation, I would feel _____.

I know I can always reach out to _____.

From this brief conversation it is difficult to be sure what is happening to Bob. Changes in a person's usual behavior and mood patterns that do not seem appropriate to what is happening in his life can be signs of deeper mental health concerns.

Depression and other mental health dysfunctions are extreme variations of normal behavior. Since normal behavior involves your mind, brain, and nervous system, mental dysfunctions often entangle these components in complex ways.

The ways in which you relate as partners involve your perceptions, interpretations, emotions, decisions, and actions. When these aspects do not function well, your marriage relationship is affected. For example, being excessively or anxiously concerned about yourself may be related to emotional malnourishment. Temper outbursts, excessive spending, and seeking attention may be signs of an underlying emotional dysfunction.

A sense of general distress, inadequacy, and depression may occur along with these disorders or independent of them. A person may feel discouraged or demoralized, which may appear in marriage as a general feeling of failure due to a belief by one partner that the marriage will not work. Loss of motivation, initiative, and energy may appear in emotional aloofness and withdrawal. Wide mood swings, depression, or anger especially affects marriage because it is easy for the other partner to assume that he or she is somehow causing the depression or anger.

When personality changes concern you or your spouse, one important step is to obtain professional consultation. Some of these sources are described in Part 7.

THE ROOTS OF PERSONALITY CHANGES

Consider a mental health disorder that you face. Based on your personal knowledge and history, in what ways are each of these causes contributing to your situation?

Physiological, biochemical changes: _____.

Temperament, hereditary factors: _____.

Childhood and adolescence influences: _____.

Experiences before marriage: _____.

Current marital interactions: _____.

SOME SIGNS OF MENTAL HEALTH

Making the love power system work well for you and your spouse is certainly a major sign of good mental health. It is based on a Christian understanding of how God has created and redeemed us and how God continues to offer nurture to each person and marriage today.

Having good mental health in your marriage means being emotionally independent and free from parents. Having clear, flexible boundaries that allow you and your spouse to have both separateness and connectedness to parents, relatives, and friends is another sign of emotional health.

Additional signs of good mental health for me are _____.

They help us in our marriage in these ways: _____.

P

L O V E

W

E

R

The LORD is the strength of my life;
Of whom shall I be afraid? . . .
I will sing praises to the LORD (Ps. 27:1, 6).

In a healthy home a child is surrounded by security, flexibility, challenges, and encouragements that create good mental health habits, higher self-esteem, respect for others' property and rights, and positive attitudes. Homes that have rigid or chaotic rules, inconsistent discipline patterns, or emotionally immature parents will produce children with poor mental health and emotional problems.

FAMILY EVENTS AND IMPACTS

Among your relatives (including yourself), how often have these events happened? What kind of impact has each had on you? Make one entry in each column of five blanks for each item. Then discuss your answers.

	Happened			Impact on Me	
	None	*Some*	*Often*	*Positive*	*Negative*
Divorce/separation	—	— —	— —	— —	— — —
Unresolved marital conflicts, arguments	—	— —	— —	— —	— — —
Alcohol abuse, problem drinking	—	— —	— —	— —	— — —
Abuse of drugs	—	— —	— —	— —	— — —
Participation in church and/or other groups	—	— —	— —	— —	— — —

	Happened			Impact on Me		
	None	Some	Often	Positive		Negative
Physical abuse and/or threats	—	—	—	—	—	—
Sexual abuse and/or threats	—	—	—	—	—	—
Financial problems, loss of credit	—	—	—	—	—	—
Violence toward others and/or self	—	—	—	—	—	—
Family meals and/or special times together	—	—	—	—	—	—
Problems in school, school dropouts	—	—	—	—	—	—
Loss of jobs, unable to find work	—	—	—	—	—	—
Major illnesses, accidents, bad health	—	—	—	—	—	—
Physical disabilities	—	—	—	—	—	—
Closeness to friends and relatives	—	—	—	—	—	—
Early deaths, other major losses	—	—	—	—	—	—
Moved often, many major changes	—	—	—	—	—	—
Extramarital affairs and/or sexual problems	—	—	—	—	—	—

Chapter 24

Extramarital Sexual Affairs and Sex Addictions

In the middle of dinner at one of their favorite restaurants, Maria commented, "You remember Liz at work? Well, today she told me she has been having an affair with her boss. That creates all kinds of problems."

"Yeah, it would," replied Carlos. "Sounds like Harry. He's always involved with some woman, and he is worried that his wife and the other woman's husband will find out."

"I'm so glad we don't have to worry about that," smiled Maria. "We must be doing something right."

Extramarital affairs are about more than physical sex. Extramarital sexual relationships carry a variety of meanings for a couple. Among these are a need for reassurance, emotional acceptance, and companionship. Affairs may also happen when there is a mismatch between spouses' sexual appetites or when one partner uses an affair as revenge or as a cry for help.

Sometimes current stresses add to sex addictions, sexual disorders, and unresolved issues from childhood and adolescence to produce extramarital affairs. Sex addiction occurs when a person misuses sexual activities for nurturing that would normally be obtained through healthy family, friendship, and work relationships. Although sexual dysfunctions may involve other persons in addition to the one with the disorder, unresolved developmental needs can be acted out in sexual ways.

Another person cannot cause you or your spouse to become sexually involved outside your marriage unless some unresolved predisposing conditions are already present in your marriage. Extramarital affairs are emotional reactions expressed through sexual channels.

Some emotions that affairs might express are _____.

Influences that could add
up to produce an affair are _____.

AFTER AN AFFAIR

If an extramarital affair is not a problem in your marriage, celebrate what you are doing to maintain a good marriage, leaving no room for intruders. In the next section of this chapter you may review the positives that "affair proof" your marriage.

One reason affairs are not a problem for us is _____.

If you are already coping effectively and positively with an extramarital affair, you are probably applying the principles described here. Review what you have done and are doing to achieve this good result. Thank your spouse, and keep affirming each other in your progress.

How my spouse and I are
now coping with this situation: _____.

If an extramarital affair is a negative factor in your marriage, you need to resolve it constructively now. Affairs are exits through which you escape learning to love in your marriage. There are several steps to cope with an affair.

1. If you are having the affair, learn what it means to you so you can honestly decide to stop it. You may stop the extramarital liaison because you are afraid of discovery, a sexually transmitted disease, or pregnancy. However, these constraints do not address your deeper needs that led to the affair.

How I will stop this affair: _____.

Some deeper needs that led up to it: _____.

2. If you suspect your spouse is involved in an affair or other intimate friendship that seems inappropriate or makes you feel uncomfortable, become aware of all of your feelings. Initially, you may feel hurt, angry, rejected, embarrassed, and/or inadequate. You may want to blame your spouse, get revenge, withdraw sexually, and/or heap guilt and rejection on your spouse.

You may also be tempted to contact the other person in your spouse's extramarital liaison. You may feel like inflicting harm on that person.

All these are typical reactions, yet they will not resolve the affair. Since you cannot solve the affair with these responses, recognize the feelings, but be sure you stop any impulsive actions that will only make the situation worse.

Why I think my spouse is having this affair: _____.

How I feel about it: _____.

3. Explore deeper in yourself to discover how you and your spouse have contributed to the affair and what each is willing to do now that you know about the affair. For this step both need professional consultation.

If your spouse will go with you to find help, be grateful and do it. Even if you are the only one who has concerns, go by yourself to get help.

Sources for effective help with this situation: _____.

How I (or we) will use these helps: _____.

4. Describe clearly what you want to happen after the affair is over. What was each missing in your marriage that led up to the affair? You probably do not want to go back to the "old" marriage, so you can specify what you want your marriage to become.

What I want our marriage to be: _____.

5. Forgive and reconcile, putting the affair in the past and starting afresh in your marriage. Look for the positive qualities. Acknowledge the pain, hurt, and other feelings. Listen and care for each other. As God forgives and reconciles you, let the Holy Spirit heal you, your spouse, and your relationship.

These and other aspects of reconciliation and renewal are difficult but not impossible. Together you can do it with support.

In this situation the difficult work is _____.

How I feel about doing these steps is _____.

HOW TO AFFAIR PROOF YOUR MARRIAGE

When a relationship becomes more than just a friendly one, it may become an extramarital sexual affair. The most effective protection against these difficult situations is to have so many positives in your marriage that there is no emotional emptiness that other relationships might fill.

Concerning sexual areas, we need these positive patterns: _____.

How we will create and keep them going in our marriage: _____.

You also maintain sexual fidelity when you and your spouse set your own ground rules for sexual activities, just as you set guides for spending money or structuring time. You probably assume that you may have friendships with persons of either sex but that sexual intercourse or other explicit sexual activities are not permitted.

Talk openly with each other about what these friendships can and cannot involve, including time, sex, money, and influence. In this way you cooperatively set your guidelines concerning sexual activities. You can also support each other in modifying them as needed throughout your marital journey.

Some essential sexual guidelines are _____.

Whether something is a crisis depends upon your moral standards and understandings as a couple.

Agreements concerning sex I have for myself are _____.

Sexual understandings I have for my spouse are _____.

> **P**
> **L O V E**
> **O**
> **W**
> **E**
> **R**
>
> *Let the husband give appropriate affection to his wife, and likewise the wife give affection to her husband. The husband affects how his wife responds sexually, and the wife affects how her husband responds sexually. Do not withhold sexual affection unless you mutually consent for fasting and prayer, then come together to strengthen each other (based on 1 Cor. 7:3-5).*

A malnourished husband or wife sets the stage for many damages to the marriage as well as to the marriages and families of others. Sexual acting out occurs when the lonely wife or husband turns to a friend or neighbor for the affirmation and affection really wanted from the spouse.

In inappropriate sexual situations each person involved can take action.

How I would cope with an
inappropriate sexual situation: _____.

172 DECREASING YOUR NEGATIVES

POSITIVE INTIMACY

Positive intimacy means that you and your spouse experience the balance of togetherness and separateness. You can be close to each other without feeling smothered or enmeshed or losing your personal space boundaries. You can also be separate individuals with each other without feeling isolated or abandoned or losing positive times together.

Each partner has an image of intimacy. Compare these images so you can clarify what each expects concerning intimacy in your marriage.

For me, intimacy means _____.

I feel too close and smothered when _____.

I feel too far away and abandoned when _____.

For my spouse, intimacy means _____.

My spouse feels too close and smothered when _____.

My spouse feels too far away and abandoned when _____.

Chapter 25

Alcohol Abuse

Suppose your spouse said, "Honey, I don't feel so well. I think I'll have another drink. Please call the boss and tell him I'm sick today."

How would you reply?

"Okay. You just rest, and I'll do all the work around here. What else can I do to make you feel better?"

"Nobody respects you. If you take another drink, I'm leaving."

"Call your boss yourself. You're in better shape than I am."

"I want you to feel better, and I want us to change this pattern."

In this circumstance, how
would you answer your spouse? _____

What hopes or concerns would you have? _____

Usually a symptom of underlying hurts and pain, alcohol abuse affects the marriage system in many ways. Whether one or both spouses abuse alcoholic beverages, or even if one or both spouses come from families where alcohol was (or is) a problem, both spouses are involved.

The actions of the person who abuses alcohol negatively impact both partners. Typically, the abuser places alcohol above spouse and family, which distorts the marriage relationship. The abuser increasingly depends upon alcohol to deaden the pain of emotional hurts and provide relief from stresses of many kinds. The abusing spouse often expects others to accommodate his or her wishes.

The other spouse usually modifies attitudes and actions (knowingly or not) to accommodate the spouse's alcohol abuse. As the abuser's use of alcohol affects job performance and family relationships, the nonabusing partner takes more control of the family.

Because the cycle of abuse deepens as each partner changes in response to the other partner's actions, positive changes in one partner can break the abuse cycle and free both spouses to find constructive solutions.

Definitions of *alcoholic* and *alcoholism* vary. In relation to marriage, the most useful assumption is that when use of beverage alcohol creates a problem for you, your spouse, and/or others, you have a problem with alcohol.

What I mean by alcohol use or abuse: _____.

How this alcohol use affects me: _____.

How alcohol use has affected my spouse: _____.

How I feel about answering these statements: _____.

Alcohol abuse is an unsuccessful effort to cope with personal and marital difficulties that are painful and overwhelming. Assessment and diagnosis of alcohol abuse are complex. Full treatment requires much skill, energy, and time to maintain sobriety and heal the deeper dysfunctions out of which the alcohol abuse originated.

The love power solution begins when you admit that your pattern of alcohol use and/or that of your spouse and/or others you love create problems for you. Admitting that you have an alcohol-related problem is the first step to treatment. This admission applies whether you use alcohol or not. Alcohol may be the most dominant invisible "person" in your marriage or family. Unrecognized, it gains even more power to disrupt and destroy a marriage.

A major unseen negative force in our marriage is _____.

My part in allowing this to happen is _____.

What I want to do about this is _____.

THREE ALCOHOL ABUSE OPTIONS

1. If you do not have any problem with alcohol, and you can independently verify this with your spouse and others who know you, this chapter may enable you to be sensitive to the impact of alcohol on millions of homes and families. Perhaps you can join sobriety, health, and wholeness. Part 8 provides some suggestions.

May God lead you to find and implement effective ways to cope with the consequences of alcohol abuse by others.

I will help others cope with
alcohol abuse in these ways: _____.

2. If you are now coping effectively and positively with alcohol abuse, you are probably already positively addressing the problems described in this chapter. May God continue to bless you in your progress toward healing, health, and joy.

I will continue to cope positively
with alcohol abuse in these ways: _____.

3. If you have alcohol-related concerns about yourself or your spouse, get help now. This advice is the best recommendation this chapter can give you. May God enable you to find positive solutions to current alcohol-related issues.

If your spouse will go with you to find help, be thankful and get going. If your spouse will not seek help, then seek help by yourself. Even if you are the only one who sees alcohol abuse concerns, go by yourself to get help. Check Part 7 for possible sources of help. May you know God's safety and guidance as you proceed.

I will take these steps to find
positive solutions to the alcohol-
related issues in which I am involved: _____.

Of these three alcohol abuse possibilities, I mostly fit in option _____.

Some steps I can take are _____.

Chapter 26

Food Abuses, Diets, and Weight

"How to take off fifty pounds in fifty days."

"If you don't lose weight, I'm leaving."

"For a new you and a new body, join our club and buy our products."

"My weight protects me from getting hurt by sex and intimacy."

"Food has taken over my life. Food is my lover."

"Inside this big body is a lonely, hurting child."

"If only I were not so overweight, my husband would love me."

"I binge and purge about once a week. Isn't that normal?"

"Food is the only part of my life I have been able to control, but now it controls me."

These statements represent some of the complicated factors that turn eating into a problem. Eating disorders such as excessive dieting, bulimia, and anorexia usually express deeper psychological and family conflicts that also disrupt a marriage. How familiar are these statements to you and your spouse?

Most of these statements are _____.

In our marriage food means _____.

In addition to essential nutrition, good food is a major dimension of daily life, family celebrations, and social gatherings. Weight gain and loss may accompany changes in your health, your routine, or other areas of your life and marriage.

These are normal, and you adjust to them, perhaps with difficulty, but without becoming obsessed with food and appearance.

For some persons, family distress, social pressures, and physiological factors can combine to change a normal healthy food use into an answer to intense loneliness and loss. The potential for food abuses is amplified with society's extreme emphasis on physical and sexual attractiveness. Eating becomes an occasion for family members to fight over who can control each person's life.

Are there ways in which eating has become a control issue with you, your spouse, and relatives? If so, what are they? _____

How do you use food to solve emotional needs? _____

SOME SOURCES OF FOOD ABUSES IN MARRIAGE

Eating disorders and other food abuses express deeper pain and loneliness that you can heal and satisfy in your marriage with your spouse.

Loneliness and loss result from feeling rejected and abandoned.

Times I feel lonely are _____.

Times my spouse feels lonely are _____.

Ways we can nurture each other are _____.

Guilt and self-blame occur when the lonely person somehow assumes that negative family tensions are her or his fault. This may lead to the "if only" trap in which the lonely person says, "If only I would lose weight, my spouse would respect me and love me."

P
L O V E
W
E
R

Where the Spirit of the Lord is, there is liberty (2 Cor. 3:17).

Repressed anger and rage, if unresolved, can lead to depression and/or to violence. Becoming aware of these old painful emotions in a safe and supportive relationship, such as marriage, is a major part of the healing process for eating disorders.

Something that really makes me upset is _____.

Some sources of my anger and rage are _____.

Ways I cope with anger and rage are _____.

STEPS TOWARD CHANGE

Treatment for food-related abuses begins when you admit you have a problem and you want to change. If you have the problem, ask your spouse to support and affirm you as you seek to change. If your spouse has the problem, be clear in declaring your love, and be open to finding answers and solutions.

A food-related concern I have is _____.

Support I need for food changes includes _____.

You can begin now with your spouse to increase your emotional and spiritual nurture and free food to be what God intended, nourishment for your physical bodies.

I am confident God helps me because _____.

Ways my spouse helps me are _____.

Ways I help my spouse in these areas are _____.

I will give appreciation to my spouse by _____.

Chapter 27

Drug Abuses

"I don't abuse drugs, but every few weeks I do like to get high."

"My physician gave me this medicine to calm me down and that one to get me up and going each day and this other one to keep me from being depressed."

"Since I got that pill to keep me awake, I've been able to do a lot more work, but I don't feel as well as I used to."

You can become psychologically dependent on any drug, whether over the counter, legally prescribed, or illegal. In addition, your body adapts to the presence of drugs in your system, which makes you physiologically addicted. In some cases you need higher and higher doses to obtain the same apparent result from the drug.

Substance abuse effects and treatments are similar for illegal and legal drugs. Unlike legal drugs, however, illegal drugs bring major additional complications such as unpredictable side effects, legal risks, and criminal penalties.

God made your brain mysteriously complex, yet wonderfully efficient. Science is just beginning to understand the intricate and delicate balances between the brain and the nervous system's physiological structure, biochemical functions, and electrochemical operation. Your mind and spirit interact with these physical structures to produce the integrated results of perceiving, thinking, feeling, deciding, and acting. You are a unique being, a temple of God.

The strongest drug I now use is _____.

My feelings about using medicines and drugs are _____.

You probably pay little attention to your brain and body when your system is working normally. Things quickly change when you add a harmful drug to it.

A drug-related change I have experienced is _____.

How I felt (or feel) about it was _____.

How it affects our marriage now is _____.

Some changes I want to make are _____.

YOUR DECISIONS ABOUT DRUG ABUSE

If drug abuse is no problem for you and your spouse, describe how your positive patterns keep you drug free and mentally healthy. You might explore how you can enable others to develop these positives.

The way my spouse and I continue drug-free patterns is _____.

One way we can enable drug-free living for others is _____.

If you had drug-related problems in the past, celebrate your strengths and resources for making and maintaining these changes.

Resources and strengths I have now are _____.

The way my spouse and I maintain drug-free patterns is _____.

ELEMENTS OF TREATMENT FOR SUBSTANCE ABUSE

If you have a substance abuse concern for yourself or your spouse, the first step toward healing is to believe that change is possible and then decide to change. Treatment for substance abuse requires well-trained professional help.

A decision to change your life that is founded upon a personal experience with God is vital. Even when you feel uncertain about your desire for change, this spiritual redirection can be the anchor and foundation to which you can always return.

My decision is firm and clear because _____.

Physical withdrawal from the substance must usually be under medical guidance because your body must readjust to not having the drug. Depending on many factors, these withdrawal symptoms and changes will take several days or weeks to stabilize.

The way I will achieve safe withdrawal
from the abused substance(s) is _____.

Treatment of health conditions related to the substance abuse includes providing safe chemical substitutes for the abusive substances, diet changes, and proper health routines in your daily life. Medical treatment may also be needed to counteract damage to organs and nerve system components.

<table>
<tr><td>
P
L O V E
W
E
R
</td><td>
Then they cried to the Lord in their trouble, and God delivered them from their distress. Let us thank the Lord for His steadfast love and wonderful works for all persons (based on Ps. 107:28, 31).
</td></tr>
</table>

Related health conditions that need medical treatment are _____.

Supportive persons provide encouragement for changes.

Supportive persons for me are _____.

Counseling allows you to become aware of some of the causes of your abuse.

Goals and progress in counseling are _____.

Rectifying damages done to others because of your abuse involves setting things right wherever you can, provided it does more good than harm.

Repairs and restitutions I need to make are _____.

Learning new positive patterns in marriage may be done through marriage counseling, marriage enrichment, consultation with friends and relatives, reading, and other ways. These can help you and your spouse to discriminate between negative and positive patterns and practice the positives with accurate, helpful, encouraging feedback and guidance.

Some new patterns we are learning are _____.

Long-term involvement in social network supports is essential.

Support networks my spouse and I value are _____.

Chapter 28

Gambling Addictions

"Maybe my luck will change."

"If we win the lottery, we will be able to pay our bills."

"Uh, I don't know what happened, but I bet the rent money on a sure winner and lost."

"I skipped work in order to go to the races."

Statements like these may be made when gambling is a problem in a marriage. With increased legalized gambling opportunities and advertising that suggests that gambling is desirable, more marriages will be affected by difficulties and addictions related to gambling.

The primary attraction of gambling is the hope, however remote, of getting a desirable prize of money or goods in exchange for little or no effort.

Gambling in all forms only works when many persons pay into a pool from which one or a few are randomly chosen to win most of the pool of money. The fundamental principle of gambling is that in order for one person to win many others must lose.

Gambling is a moral issue. If one believes that any attempt to get something without earning it is wrong, all forms of gambling, whether legal or not, are unacceptable. From this view gambling is the same as stealing from others. Moral principles of honest work for honest pay, making informed choices, and taking responsibility for one's actions lead one to reject all forms of gambling.

GAMBLING IN YOUR MARRIAGE

You and your spouse must decide what constitutes gambling for you. One option is to agree together that all gambling is wrong. Another option is to decide on certain gambling activities you will participate in and fix a maximum amount that you will spend. When you reach that amount, you stop the gambling activities. In either option, agreeing on the moral principles involved for you is essential.

What activities do you or your
spouse consider gambling? _____

In which of these activities will you
participate? What limits will you set? _____

In what ways have gambling patterns caused
disagreements or difficulties in your marriage? _____

How have you coped with these difficulties? _____

WHEN GAMBLING BECOMES A PROBLEM

Gambling becomes a problem for you when it is out of control or when you and your spouse disagree about gambling. Gambling may be encouraged when one spouse unknowingly increases the pressure for expensive possessions and activities.

Gambling becomes an addiction when a person gambles money that is needed for basic necessities or becomes obsessed with the thrill of taking a risk, regardless of the consequences. Sometimes this risk taking may not be noticed by anyone other than the addicted person.

More subtle signs of possible gambling addiction include impulse buying, reckless driving, shoplifting, and unauthorized borrowing (embezzlement) with the hope that the money can be repaid before anyone discovers it is missing.

If you find it difficult to avoid gambling and/or taking other dangerous high risks, your first step is to decide that it is a problem. Next steps include talking with your spouse about possible solutions and getting professional help to control or eliminate the gambling activities.

When taking risks seems out of my control: _____.

What I need to do: _____.

If gambling is not a problem in your marriage, discover the reasons and continue to use positives to crowd out troublesome risk taking.

How we avoid taking unnecessary risks: _____.

Ways we could help others control
or avoid gambling addictions: _____.

P
L O V E   *The LORD knows the way of the righteous,*
W   *But the way of the ungodly shall perish*
E   *(Ps. 1:6).*
R

Chapter 29

Violence

"Wife kills husband who had been abusing her for fifteen years."

"Of persons convicted of crime, 85 percent were physically abused as children."

"If your spouse hits the wall, throws things, and kicks the dog, watch out because you are probably next."

"What is your escape plan in case your spouse becomes violent?"

"Violence is the weapon of last resort."

Violence is the weapon of last resort that people use when they cannot reach their goals any other way. A person who feels trapped or cornered will use violence if other resources and skills fail. This happens in marriage as well as in other close relationships.

Violence is hurting people hurting people. Much of the violence in our society was learned in violent homes where parents fought with each other, severely punished their children, and taught disrespect for persons and property. When you hurt someone, that person will pass that hurt to someone else. When you love someone, that person will pass that love to someone else.

Every home should be a safe sanctuary for peace and protection, but many homes are dangerous to spouses and children. As husband and wife, you control the safety of your home.

TYPES OF FAMILY VIOLENCE

Violence between spouses and between family members appears in many forms. Pushing, shoving, hitting, biting, slapping, spanking, and other hurtful physical acts of aggression are the most obvious forms of domestic violence. The use of guns, knives, and other weapons is an extreme demonstration of domestic violence.

Verbal abuse is violence. Mean words do hurt men and women. Any effort to intimidate, frighten, or force your spouse in some way is violence.

Neglect is passive violence. Failing to keep promises or provide the basics of safety, shelter, food, and clothing for your family is a form of passive violence.

Inappropriate sexual activities with family members are expressions of violence. Threats of harm may be used to keep these activities secret, adding further damage to all family members.

Which forms of violence have you experienced? _____

My reactions to these types of violence are _____.

The way I will get help is _____.

Concerns I have about domestic violence are _____.

If you know of family violence among your relatives or friends, consult with your spouse or other trusted family members to find the safest effective way to stop the violence and get help to those who are involved.

Ways I can help make homes safe from violence are _____.

RATE YOUR MARRIAGE

The following exercise is difficult and possibly dangerous. If it is too threatening to discuss with your spouse, find a competent friend or professional person with whom you can talk about possible ways you can cope constructively with the negatives.

> **P**
> **L O V E**
> **W**
> **E**
> **R**
>
> *There is no fear in love; but perfect love casts out fear (1 John 4:18).*
> *When a husband loves his wife, she is safe and not afraid. When a wife loves her husband, he is safe and not afraid.*

You and your spouse can individually rate your marriage. Then talk about how the strengths you now have crowd out the negatives. If you see some negatives, describe what they are and how you are willing to do your part to change them.

How I feel about rating our marriage: _____.

How my spouse feels about this kind of rating: _____.

Place a mark on each line to show where you think your marriage is along each dimension.

Marriage Disruptions		Marriage Strengths
Anxious withdrawal	├──┼──┼──┼──┼──┤	Safe, secure intimacy
Physical, sexual abuse	├──┼──┼──┼──┼──┤	Trust through touch
Alcohol, drug abuse	├──┼──┼──┼──┼──┤	Flexible cooperation
Sexual acting out	├──┼──┼──┼──┼──┤	Sexual integrity
Eating disorders	├──┼──┼──┼──┼──┤	Mealtime sociability
Personal disintegration	├──┼──┼──┼──┼──┤	Wholeness, identity
Pain, anxiety, uncertainty	├──┼──┼──┼──┼──┤	Joy, peace, confidence
Fear of family system	├──┼──┼──┼──┼──┤	Hope for family system
Other: _____	├──┼──┼──┼──┼──┤	Other: _____

Add comments about any of these topics
as they affect your marriage now. _____

Ultimately, all negatives are a matter of spirit, decision, and attitude. You have the power to choose positives or negatives. Choose to learn the positives and experience the joyful blessings that come to you and your spouse.

> **P**
> **L O V E**
> **O**
> **W**
> **E**
> **R**
>
> *Be of one mind, having compassion for one another; . . . be tenderhearted, be courteous; not returning evil for evil (1 Pet. 3:8–9).*

Part 6

CONNECTING THE FOUR LOVE POWER DIMENSIONS

Increasing your skills for communicating love

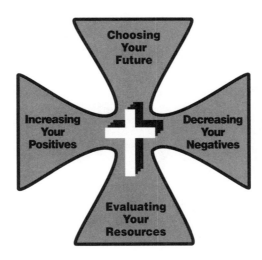

As a couple, you are constantly connecting these four dimensions—choosing your future, increasing your positives, evaluating your resources, and decreasing your negatives—in the ways you live out your marriage. You make these connections at many levels, both verbal and nonverbal. Through these connections, you make the four love power dimensions into the communion, or common union, of your marriage journey.

Some nonverbal communications I like are _____.

Some verbal styles of communicating I like are _____.

Some important connections for me are _____.

Some important connections for my spouse are _____.

These connections make our marriage better in these ways: _____.

Chapter 30

The How and What of Your Communication

Imagine that you are having a telephone conversation with a friend, but there is much static on the line. Although you both want to talk and are talking clearly, you may not hear each other well because of the static. You comment, "That was a poor conversation," meaning only that you had difficulty hearing each other. This refers to the *how* of communication.

Imagine another time when you have a very clear telephone connection. This time you are talking about a difficult topic with a difficult person and the outcome is not what you wanted. You comment, "That was a poor conversation." Here, however, you are making a value judgment about the content of the conversation. This is the *what* of communication.

Communication is both a skill (how) and a content (what). The content is what you want to communicate to your spouse so that you achieve a shared meaning. The four love power dimensions are the content (or the what) of your communication. Communication skills are how you send and receive those messages.

INTENT VERSUS IMPACT: A MAJOR KEY TO MARRIAGE SUCCESS

Accurate communication means that your message actually did impact your spouse in the way you intended. When your intent matches the impact your spouse received, your communication is accurate. The impact on your spouse may be happy or sad, welcome or not, yet if your intent matches the impact on your spouse, you have accurate communication.

A time when my message impacted
my spouse in the way I wanted: _____.

A time when my spouse's message
impacted me in the way he or she wanted: _____.

Results for our marriage were: _____.

SHARED MEANINGS DEFINE YOUR MARRIAGE

A conversation is a series of messages with each person at times being the speaker and at other times being the listener. A shared meaning happens when both speaker and listener agree on the content and impact of the message. Shared meanings that you both want are essential for success in your marriage.

Accurate communication becomes more complex when you are dealing with your relationship to each other. Although you know that the person you married is your spouse, at times you may think that he or she is acting like your parent. Uncovering associations and memories will help you to clarify your communication and free you to express positives.

A time when my spouse acted like
my mother or father or someone else: _____.

In this situation what I think might
have been happening in my spouse was _____

If you have courage, you can ask your spouse to complete the above statements as she or he sees you. You may also get some insights by noting when your spouse acts or responds as though she or he were responding to you as a parent or child.

A time when I acted like a mother or
father or someone else to my spouse: _____.

In this situation what my spouse might
have thought was happening in me was _____.

The impact this had on my spouse was _____.

THE THREE STEPS TO SHARED MEANINGS

Sending a message to your partner is the first step in accurate communication. To get a shared meaning, you also need *listener feedback* and *confirmation by the speaker.* These three components of a message enable you to know if the impact on the listener is the impact the speaker wanted.

The speaker must put the message into words and gestures that are also meaningful to the listener. Then the listener repeats back (summarizes) the speaker's message. In reply the speaker confirms that the listener's feedback is accurate. At this point both persons have a shared meaning.

The actual impact of your message shows in your partner's response to your message, as expressed in words, tone, body language, and action.

Try applying this message skill to a message you would like to share with your spouse.

Message content:
My message is (*for instance,*
"Let's stay home tonight"): _____.

Message intent:
My intent is (*for instance,*
"I enjoy being with you"): _____.

Feedback:
Then I will check to see if my partner
understands me (*for instance, "Please*
let me know what you think I am saying"): _____.

Partner's description of impact:
Summary from my partner: _____.

Confirmation:
I will let my partner know how close the
summary is to what I intended (*for*
instance, "that's it," or "you got it"): _____.

Confirmation that the impact is
what I intended (*for instance, with a*
smile, "I'm glad you got my message"): _____.

P
L O V E
W
E
R

Good communication means that the
impact on the listener matches what the
speaker intended.

Now do this process again with your spouse as the speaker and you as the listener.

PERSPECTIVES ON YOUR SPOUSE: VALUING AND CONNECTING

If you have hiked a mountain or wooded trail, you know that there are places along the trail when you can't see all that is ahead of you. When you come to a clearing, switchback, or other vantage point, you can see a much larger part of the trail ahead as well as behind you.

Whatever your speed, over a day you can see progress that you have made when you reach the vista viewpoint. You may be surprised at how far you have traveled or pleased about reaching your hiking goals.

Just as you've experienced on the trail, at times you may feel as if you are not going anyplace in your marriage. You can choose to give up, or you can take a different perspective according to the future you choose and the resources you have.

What I see in our marriage trail: _____.

The values you affirm about your future as individuals and as a couple give you perspective on your communication process.

Some ways I value my spouse: _____.

Some ways I feel valued by my spouse: _____.

How these values affect our communication now: _____.

Some of the progress we have made is _____.

Some steps we have learned are _____.

A goal I want to reach is _____.

My first step will be _____.

A later step could be _____.

Chapter 31

Listening Skills for Receiving Messages

"Your husband always seems so polite and considerate," commented Betty as Sue's husband left.

"That means a lot to me," Sue replied. "I try to make it easy for him to listen."

"That must help." Pausing, Betty sighed. "When I ask my husband if he loves me, he thinks I'm asking for information."

Listening is much more than hearing with your ears. To listen, you use your senses to receive data about what your partner is experiencing.

What do you think Betty wanted from her husband? _____

How do you feel about listening to your spouse? _____

P
L O V E   *Listening is your ability to focus on the*
O   *speaker so you understand accurately*
W   *what the speaker has said.*
E
R

BASICS OF LISTENING

Careful listening to your spouse requires at least these elements.

1. *Decide to listen.* For the moment the most important thing you can do is to listen to your spouse and try to understand and feel what your spouse wants to share with you. Love is wanting to listen to your spouse.

2. *Put aside distractions.* Lay down your reading, turn off the television, and stop doing anything else that might distract you from listening to your spouse. If you cannot do that, agree on a specific time and place when you can put everything else aside with no interruptions or distractions.

3. *Focus on the speaker.* Turn toward your spouse as the speaker. Look at your spouse. Notice facial expressions, tone of voice, and body language. If it is helpful, gently hold your spouse's hand or give other supportive and encouraging touches.

4. *Summarize often.* When you think your spouse has completed a thought, politely stop your spouse and summarize what you heard. Giving your feedback summary enables your spouse to confirm that your summary is generally accurate.

5. *Clarify if needed.* As the listener, ask brief questions only to clarify something your spouse is saying. Don't use questions to insert your viewpoints. Later when you are the speaker, you can give your opinions about what your spouse as speaker has said.

6. *Distinguish between speaker's views and your views.* Frame your listener summaries and questions with "I hear you saying," or "If I understand you correctly, you . . ." "You" messages, such as "You are mad or sad," are your views of your partner. As listener, you want to understand your spouse's views, regardless of whether you agree or disagree.

7. *Reverse listener and speaker impacts as needed.* Distinguish between message's impact on you and the next intended impact you want your reply to have on the speaker. Don't plan your comments while your spouse is speaking. When both of you are sure you have a shared meaning, you become the speaker, and the speaker becomes the listener.

Of these steps, the one that is easiest for me is _____.

Of these steps, the one that is most difficult for me is _____.

RATING YOUR LISTENING SKILLS

Think of a specific situation when you wanted to listen to your spouse. How well did you perform each of these component skills involved in listening?

Rate yourself on this scale:

>1—Listener was not aware of this as being important.
>2—Listener was aware of this but did not do it at all.
>3—Listener did this some but not enough for the situation.
>4—Listener did this adequately.
>5—Listener did this exceptionally well.

_____ 1. I put other thoughts in the background so I could give full attention to my spouse's message.

_____ 2. I turned and faced my spouse.

_____ 3. I placed my emotional reactions aside so that I could become fully aware of the emotional feelings of my spouse.

_____ 4. When I lost track of an important message, I asked my spouse to stop and repeat the message.

_____ 5. Even if I realized I was disagreeing with my spouse, I tried to receive the message accurately so that I could repeat it correctly.

_____ 6. At times I repeated my interpretation of the message so that my spouse could confirm that I was understanding it accurately.

_____ 7. I encouraged my spouse to share the complete message by indicating my willingness to listen.

_____ 8. When my spouse paused or was unable to find the exact word or phrase, I waited patiently, adding words or phrases only if my spouse requested me to do so.

_____ 9. I kept my spouse informed of my listening quotient by reporting that I was willing to continue listening or that I wanted to reverse roles so that I could send a message or that I was unable to listen more.

_____ 10. Other listening skill: _____.

If you and your spouse can do so comfortably, ask your spouse to rate you on the same items, and then compare your ratings.

SOME IFS FOR GROWTH IN LISTENING

You might tape-record a brief conversation when accurate listening is especially important and rate yourselves as listeners and as speakers. (A similar rating scale for the speaker is in the next chapter.)

After practicing the steps outlined in this chapter, you may continue to have difficulty understanding each other. If so, check these possibilities.

Hidden agendas may block good listening. You may be angry or fearful.

Stresses and strains may drain your energy and time for listening. Good listening takes as much energy as good speaking. If you are tired or feel pressured to do other urgent tasks besides listening, your concentration will be poor.

Power plays make you and your spouse competitors.

Language skill differences between you and your spouse may make listening more difficult. If one partner uses many complicated words and sentences but the other prefers a few simple words, neither will be very open to listening to the other.

Negative factors as described in Part 5 usually block or decrease accurate listening and speaking.

When these factors continue to reduce listening abilities in your relationship, you and your spouse probably will need appropriate professional help to identify and resolve the difficulties.

P
L O V E
W
E
R

To listen to your partner, you must first listen to yourself.

Chapter 32

Speaker Skills for Sending Messages

"I gave some flowers to my wife," Jim commented to Tom as they passed the flower shop on their way to lunch. "You know what she said?"

"What? 'Thanks'? 'How romantic'?" Tom guessed.

"She asked if I really loved her," Jim groaned in disbelief. "Of course I love her. That's why I gave the flowers to her."

"When was the last time you told her you loved her?" questioned Tom.

"Aw, I don't know," Jim murmured. "She should know. Look how hard I work for her and the kids. I act out my love. Talk is cheap."

"Well, since talk is such a bargain, try telling her in words as well and see what happens," Tom suggested. "It does wonders for my wife and for me."

Perhaps both Tom and Jim are correct. Communication does involve both words and actions, including your nonverbal body language that accompanies your verbal statements. Words are a special major part of communication.

What do you think Jim will do? How might Tom's marriage be different from Jim's marriage?

What Jim could say to his wife: _____.

For my spouse and me, talk is _____.

After I say "I love you," I _____.

Communication is the connection between the four love power dimensions of marriage: future, resources, positives, and negatives. Sending and receiving messages are the two halves of communication.

Sending a message is expressing who you are, what you want or think, how you feel, and what you are doing (or intend to do). In this chapter focus on the verbal messages you send to your spouse.

TWO MESSAGE LEVELS

Every message has at least two levels: (1) content or information, and (2) request or command. For example, a simple statement, "It's a beautiful day today," describes the speaker's value judgment about weather conditions and also implies that the speaker requests (expects or commands) the listener to agree.

A sentence I often say to my spouse is _____.

This sentence sends this request or command: _____.

My spouse thinks I am requesting _____.

You are more likely to be aware of your spouse's implicit requests (or commands) to you when you catch yourself thinking, "You can't tell me what to feel, think, or what I should want." Signs of implicit commands are "ought" and "should," ("you should think," or "you ought to feel").

Sometimes words express the content part of the message and body language expresses the command or request. When verbal and nonverbal channels do not agree, you are likely to believe the body language more than the words.

We can make the request open and explicit by _____.

My part in this pattern is _____.

I want us to control the pattern
so we can (continue or stop) _____.

You cannot command your spouse to be happy, just as your spouse cannot command you to be happy. You can only offer care and love that may satisfy a need or desire that you think your spouse may have.

Though I speak with the tongues of men and of angels, but have not love, I have become sounding brass or a clanging cymbal (1 Cor. 13:1).

BASICS OF SENDING MESSAGES

Expressing or sending your message includes at least these steps.

1. *Clarify your message content and request. Content* is what you want your spouse to know or feel after you have sent your message. *Request* is the response you are asking your spouse to make to your message.

A message content I want to send to my spouse is _____.

The request I am making of my spouse is _____.

I want it to have this impact: _____.

2. *Make sure your spouse is ready to listen.* Even if you are ready to speak, be sure your spouse can hear you and can focus on your message without being distracted.

A good time and place to give my spouse this message: _____.

3. *Use words that mean the same to your spouse as to you.*

Words I may need to clarify are _____.

"Red flag" words to avoid are _____.

4. *Make it easy for your spouse to listen.* Arrange the setting so both are comfortable and ready for the message.

Body language that helps send my message: _____.

Body language that detracts from
or blocks my message: _____.

5. *Invite feedback.* Send your message in small parts so your spouse can summarize each part and get confirmation that the summary is close to what you are wanting your spouse to hear.

Ways I can invite feedback from my spouse: _____.

6. *Get your listener's reactions.* Match the impact of your message on your spouse to the impact you intended your message to have.

Spouse's facial expressions and other
body language cues I will watch for reactions: _____.

7. *Thank your spouse for listening.*

Nonverbal ways I will thank my spouse for listening: _____.

Words I will use to express appreciation to my spouse: _____.

8. *Be ready to switch roles.*

Feelings I have about switching from sender to listener: _____.

Symbol or sign we will use to know which person is the sender: _____.

Communication is accurate or effective when the impact the speaker wants to have on the listener actually happens to the listener. Whether the listener really wanted to receive the speaker's impact is another story.

It is essential to distinguish accurate communication from good communication. Good or bad refers to the value or desirability of the message rather than its accuracy. You may have accurate (good) communication of a very desirable (good) impact. You may have inaccurate (poor or bad) expression of a very desirable (good or pleasant) impact.

Consider some examples in your marriage.

An undesirable message that was poorly expressed: _____.

A desirable message that was expressed unclearly: _____.

By improving expressing and listening skills, you and your spouse can eliminate most of these poorly expressed messages.

Accurate communication increases positives because each partner wants to repeat the positive again.

A desirable message that was well expressed: _____.

Action we took after the conversation: _____.

Words we used to send the desirable message: _____.

Nonverbal face and body language that added to the message: _____.

RATING EXPRESSING SKILLS FOR SPEAKING

Think about a recent situation in which you were expressing yourself or sending a message. How well did you perform these component skills?

Rate yourself on this scale:

       1—Speaker was not aware of this as being important.

       2—Speaker was aware of this but did not do it at all.

       3—Speaker did this some but not enough for the situation.

       4—Speaker did this adequately.

       5—Speaker did this exceptionally well.

_____ 1. I was completely clear about the message I wanted to send.

_____ 2. I checked with my spouse to be sure my spouse was ready before I began sending my message.

_____ 3. I sent my message in words, gestures, and body language that meant the same to my spouse as they did to me.

_____ 4. I occasionally stopped to be sure my spouse was getting my message.

_____ 5. My spouse felt comfortable asking me to clarify my message.

_____ 6. I was able to distinguish easily between the message I wanted to send and the reactions and response of my spouse to my message.

_____ 7. Other speaker skill: _____.

If you and your spouse can do so comfortably, ask your spouse to rate you on the same items, and then compare your ratings.

"I" VS "YOU" MESSAGES

"I" messages tend to bring persons closer together because they express what the sender is thinking, feeling, or wanting. "I" messages disclose what is going on inside the speaker. They describe the speaker's viewpoints and opinions.

For each of these examples of "I" statements, add your viewpoints.

I feel _____.

I think _____.

I am confident that we can _____.

I want _____.

My mother or father is _____.

I interpret this situation or action to mean _____.

"You" messages tend to push persons apart because they convey what the other person should be (or is) thinking, feeling, or wanting. As a result, "you" messages usually put the other person down or try to control that person.

Here are some examples of "you" statements followed by the modification that would make them into "I" statements.

You feel _____.

Improvement: When I see you smile, I think you are feeling happy.

You think (feel, want to) _____.

Improvement: When you say what
you do, I interpret that to mean
that you think (feel, want to) _____.

You must be crazy to _____.

Improvement: I am concerned about _____.

When you use "I" messages, both of you succeed because "I" messages clarify where you are, respect both other and self, eliminate guessing, and allow for negotiation.

Some better ways I can speak for myself are _____.

Some better ways I can assist
my spouse to speak for self are _____.

> **P**
> **L O V E**
> **W**
> **E**
> **R**
>
> *Let the words of my mouth and the*
> *meditation of my heart*
> *Be acceptable in Your sight,*
> *O LORD, my strength and my Redeemer*
> *(Ps. 19:14).*

Chapter 33

Turning Negative Messages into Positive Love Power

Conversation 1

"Recently I've been wondering about us," she says.

"Great! When do you want to go to bed?" he counters, ignoring her concern.

"All you ever think about is sex," she mind reads with criticism.

"There's nothing wrong with sex," he defends. Then with contempt, "Why don't you grow up?"

Moving farther away, she becomes silent or shouts back, then withdraws.

You can probably fill in the rest of the conversation as it spirals downward to one more step toward a broken marriage. Suppose you had this couple redo their conversation, beginning with the same starting statement.

Conversation 2

"Recently I've been wondering about us," she says.

"What about us?" he invites, asking for more information.

"Well, it's that business and vacation trip coming up," she describes.

"Is that a problem in some way?" he asks.

Moving closer, she describes her concern and then invites him to talk about what he wants, and they solve the problem.

You can probably fill in the rest of the conversation as it draws the spouses closer together and on to an increasingly satisfying marriage.

The couple in Conversation 1 let their romance wither because they did not change their patterns of negative conversations. They chose to criticize, condemn, and pull away from each other. As you can see in Conversation 2, a different response to the opening statement took that couple in a much better direction.

My reaction to Conversation 1 is _____.

Conversation 2 is better because _____.

What seems unrealistic about this is _____.

Now that you know the basics of communicating love and can use the positive skills for listening to your partner and expressing yourself to your partner, take a closer look at what you can do when your conversation seems to slide away from a positive outcome.

DECIDE TO EMPHASIZE THE POSITIVE

You begin to turn negative impacts into positive ones by deciding that you want to make your conversations different. Wanting to change enough to vow to make it better is the important first step. You cannot change your spouse, but you can change yourself.

I can't change my spouse because _____.

I can change myself in these ways: _____.

> **P**
> **L O V E**
> **W**
> **E**
> **R**
>
> *Do not be conformed to this world, but be transformed by the renewing of your mind, that you may prove what is that good and acceptable and perfect will of God (Rom. 12:2).*

REPLACE CRITICISM WITH ACCURATE FEEDBACK

When your spouse criticizes you, you probably feel put down or belittled. That hurts. Constant criticism usually leads a person to feel inadequate.

You may respond to your spouse's criticism by agreeing, retaliating, crying, or sulking. These and other similar reactions make the criticism increase. Consider when these happen.

Some situations when my spouse criticizes me are _____.

When my spouse criticizes me, I feel _____.

By changing your response to your spouse's criticism, you give your spouse accurate feedback about the impact of that criticism on you. Consider situations when your spouse criticizes you, and then create a reply that gives your partner clear information about what that does to you.

For instance, if your spouse criticizes you for something you are doing or not doing, try including these elements in your reply: "When I am driving and you criticize me, I feel hurt. I know you respect me and mean well, but I would like to find a way to receive your comments so I can use them to change. I value you, and I want you to value me."

Try these elements for yourself:

Situation: _____.

Spouse's comment you hear as criticism: _____.

Your feeling: _____.

Your affirmation of spouse: _____.

Your willingness to consider healthy changes: _____.

Although you probably do not perceive yourself as criticizing your spouse, at times your spouse might feel criticized. The impact of your comments may not be what you intended.

Suppose your spouse hears your comments as criticism. You can begin by asking your partner to identify when this happens and then invite your partner to repeat (as near as possible) the statements you make that come across as criticism.

Situation: _____.

Spouse's quotes of you that feel like criticism: _____.

Spouse's feelings in response to your "criticism": _____.

A different way your spouse would like
to have your comments in order to change: _____.

Your thanks to your spouse for this feedback: _____.

Kind, loving, and accurate feedback assumes that the receiver can change, offers an open forum for deciding which changes, and continues mutual support in making the changes.

REPLACING DEFENSIVENESS WITH OPENNESS

To enable your spouse to replace defensiveness with openness, check your statements and other behaviors to see if you are threatening your spouse in some way. You probably did not intend to hurt your partner, but nevertheless something you did or said may have come across in a hurtful or threatening way that called up defensive patterns.

What I say or do that provokes my spouse's defenses: _____.

What my spouse wants for self: _____.

Suggestions for sharing feedback with openness: _____.

Ways I affirm my spouse in this process: _____.

A situation when my spouse reports that I seem defensive: _____.

Feedback my spouse wants to give me: _____.

Possible changes I choose to make: _____.

REPLACE WITHDRAWAL WITH CLOSENESS

Flight and fight are the two major ways for coping with negative situations. Most persons pull away rather than risk losing in a fight unless they think the cost of retreating is greater than the cost of confronting the negative to correct or overcome it. This happens in marriage, also.

Withdrawal is a negative response between partners. (Retreating from your partner is not the same as planning some individual time in your marriage.)

For me, the difference between
retreating and having individual time is _____.

I feel like escaping from my spouse when _____.

Some ways I replace escape with closeness are _____.

A time when my spouse withdrew from me was _____.

The threat my spouse probably saw in me was _____.

I am willing to make it safe and less
threatening for my spouse in these ways: _____.

A time when I withdrew from my spouse _____.

I felt threatened because _____.

My spouse could make it safe
and less threatening for me in these ways: _____.

Changes my spouse and I might make are _____.

P
L O V E
O
W   *A soft answer turns away wrath,*
E   *But a harsh word stirs up anger (Prov.*
R   *15:1).*

You can choose to turn negative messages into positive love power. Change begins with your decision to change something in yourself. You cannot change your partner by demanding a change because that will sound like criticism and a command to your spouse. Your commands can only bring out your spouse's defenses.

Try some of these changes in yourself.

A change I want in our marriage: _____.

How I will change myself to
change our marriage: _____.

When I will make this change: _____.

How I will know it makes a difference: _____.

If you find that the negatives persist and the positives you seek seem just as far away, you may need to consult with a professional counselor. You can discover the reasons that your well-intentioned efforts fail to increase your marital satisfaction. You can also create ways to make the changes you want in yourself.

Chapter 34

Cooperating for Problem Solving

"Hi, honey. I'm home at last," Chuck said as he took off his coat.

"It's about time. You're late again," Marge grumbled.

Surprised, Chuck asked, "What's wrong? Aren't you glad to see me?"

"Yes and no," stammered Marge. "Being late may not be a problem for you, but it certainly is for me. I rushed home from work so we could fix dinner together, and then you didn't show up. I'm left with all the work."

"That's not what I intended," Chuck explained as he reached to hug Marge.

"Maybe not, but I want to figure out a better way," replied Marge.

"So my being late created a problem for you?" asked Chuck.

"Right!" Marge emphasized. "Let's work on it."

For Chuck, being home "at last" seemed like some type of relief from something else. He probably did not see himself as being "late again," but Marge defined it that way, which made it a problem for her. Only when Chuck could see the situation from Marge's perspective did he begin to be open to problem solving.

A situation becomes a problem when something about it prevents one or more persons from reaching goals that they want. When the barrier is outside the marriage, spouses can unite and cooperate as a team to cope with the problem. When the obstacle is something about the other spouse, it is still important for spouses to feel like a team. In both types of problems, however, you can apply the same problem-solving steps.

I see a problem as a (*for instance,*
difficulty, dilemma, quandary, obstacle) _____.

When I face a problem, I usually feel _____.

STEPS FOR SUCCESSFUL PROBLEM SOLVING

You and your spouse can apply these steps to problem situations in your marriage.

How well can you do each of these steps? Decide on one problem you can examine as you consider each step for problem solving.

1. *Describe the situation clearly.* Assume that you are a disinterested reporter who is trying to get the facts about the situation. Answer which situation, who is involved, when it happens, and what each person is saying or doing. Report the situation in terms separate from your feelings or judgments.

For example, saying that your spouse "talks too much" or "never talks" does not describe the situation. Instead, describe the specific situation so that you and your partner agree to focus on a specific circumstance.

My illustration situation is _____.

2. *Who owns which problem?* State your problem clearly. Describe specific behaviors or actions and the way they constitute a problem for you. Identify the component parts of the problem.

For instance, you might identify your problem by telling your spouse, "Last night when we were at the party together and you spent all evening talking to others, my problem was that I didn't know anyone there and I felt lonely and ignored."

My problem is _____.

Because of this problem, I feel _____.

3. *Which goal is blocked?* Clearly state the reason for the problem. You can best do this by describing how the problem blocks reaching a specific goal you want.

For instance, "At that party I wanted to meet your friends, but when you were somewhere else, you could not introduce me to them."

My goal is _____.

The behavior that prevents reaching my goal is _____.

My part in this situation is _____.

Your part in this situation is _____.

4. *Describe possible solutions.* Develop hunches about the situation and about how you might resolve your problem. Describe alternate plans for action and the probable consequences of each plan for you and for others. Identify whether you and others have the resources to make each solution happen.

For example, "At that party it would have helped if you had introduced me to one or two persons before you went over to talk to your boss, if you had stayed with me longer, or if you had told me before we went that you wanted to circulate without me."

Some possible solutions are _____.

5. *Select a solution.* From the possible answers, select one to implement. Clearly state the specific actions that you and others will do to reach the goal that the problem blocks.

For instance, "Let's agree that at the next party you will make sure I am comfortable talking to one of your friends before you circulate, and every thirty minutes or so you will check with me to see how I am doing."

The solution we will use is _____.

6. *Take action.* Do it. Apply your selected solution to the next appropriate situation. In the party example, the two spouses applied their solution to the next party both attended.

This is what we actually did: _____.

7. *Compare results to the goals you set* in Step 3. If you achieved your objective, specify exactly how and why you did. If you failed to achieve the desired outcome, return to Step 1 and do the problem-solving process again. Regardless of outcome, thank your spouse for working with you to resolve the problem.

After the next party, the spouses compared notes. One spouse reported, "It helped for you to introduce me. I liked talking with Pat, who also introduced me to some other persons." The other spouse replied, "Then it worked out fine. I was proud to introduce you, and I felt better knowing you were also having a good time while I did a bit of business with some others at the party."

Our comparison report is _____.

MAKING DECISIONS ABOUT PROBLEMS

A decision is always made before the results are available. Solutions to some problems produce very desirable outcomes, but other choices bring unexpected or unwanted consequences.

When I am in the middle of making
an important decision, I usually feel _____.

Factors that hinder my decisions about problems are _____.

My resources (such as communication
skills) influence the solutions in these ways: _____.

Helpful persons with whom
I consult about decisions are _____.

In making selections with specific
consequences, I try to consider _____.

TOWARD FLEXIBLE SOLUTIONS

Usually, there is more than one way to do something. Most problems have more than one cause. It is important to free yourself and your spouse to implement a solution independently rather than the way you require. Flexibility in applying solutions keeps you from creating additional problems about who tells whom what to do.

How I feel about my spouse and
me doing the same task differently: _____.

Ways I can build bridges for better
problem solving in our marriage: _____.

```
P
L  O  V  E
W
E
R
```

No one sews a piece of unshrunk cloth on an old garment; or else the new piece pulls away from the old, and the tear is made worse (Mark 2:21).

Chapter 35

Resolving Conflicts

"Maybe this is a problem we just can't solve," Max concluded as he looked off into the sunset.

"We're not problems to each other," encouraged Ellen. "We disagree because we are different, and we have different points of view."

Taking her hand, Max continued, "Some differences are really nice, as in sex, but some conflicts seem like they are just too much."

"We can learn to live with these differences, too," Ellen affirmed. "Let's take another look at this whole situation and find a way for each of us to get some of what we want."

"Maybe we can reduce our conflicts to acceptable differences," replied Max. "I think the first step toward a peaceful solution would be . . ."

Conflict remains when you cannot solve a problem. Conflict usually brings hurt, anger, and other negative feelings.

There are three basic ways to cope constructively with conflicts that produce negative feelings in you:

1. *Flight.* Moving away from a threatening situation puts more distance between you and it (or the threatening person). This changes your relation to the threat. Withdrawing restores personal safety by getting farther away from the threat.

2. *Fight.* This is moving against another person or situation with intent to destroy that person's ability to threaten you.

3. *Reorientation.* Some threats (and their consequent fear and anger-producing results) dissolve or disappear when you take a different look at them. Reorientation occurs, for example, when the threat of being lost disappears as you locate familiar markers or when the fear of being alone is replaced with the joy of knowing that your partner really does care about you.

In the opening dialogue Ellen and Max chose to reorient themselves to the situation that was producing conflict rather than fight each other or run away from each other.

How do you feel about the way Max
and Ellen handled their conflict? _____

Which coping responses do you
typically use with your partner
when negative feelings appear? _____

Summarize a recent incident when
you used one of these coping
mechanisms with your partner: _____.

Which of these coping behaviors
does your partner use most often? _____

Describe when your partner does this: _____.

How do you feel about the results? _____

The ways you value yourself and your partner greatly influence how you will handle conflicts.

CHOOSING TO VALUE SELF AND SPOUSE

The way you choose to cope with conflict begins with the way you choose to value both yourself and your spouse.

There are four possible combinations of values, each with its own result.

	I value you.	I do not value you.
I value myself.	*Declare* Both win.	*Demand* I win. You lose.
I do not value myself.	*Defer* I lose. You win.	*Detach* Both lose.

Declare means that you describe what you are experiencing by giving clear "I" messages. After you and your spouse know each other's viewpoints, you can negotiate some type of compromise.

When you declare, you speak for yourself and allow your spouse to speak for himself or herself. Each partner wants the best for both persons, which means that both win. Equal and balanced power models of marriage encourage a declare-declare relationship between spouses. When you declare, you show your love to your spouse as your neighbor before God.

Complete these examples of declare messages to describe yourself in relation to your spouse and your marriage:

I want _____.

I don't like _____.

I wish we could _____.

I think _____.

I feel _____.

I appreciate _____.

I am _____.

I wish the best for _____.

When you and your spouse give declare messages, both of you win.

Some declare messages
I try to give to my spouse: _____.

Some declare messages I
like to receive from my spouse: _____.

Demand means that you use some type of force to get your way. When you demand, you value yourself more than you value your partner.

Demanders may be unaware of how they are hurting others. The demander is trying to win at the expense of the spouse, who must then lose. The demander seeks to control and restrict others, which usually triggers anger, rage, and other negative reactions in the demander's spouse.

Making demands on others may be a personal style that has developed because a person has often gotten away with putting others down.

Here are some typical demanding behaviors that you might use to get your way in a conflict. Which of these "get my way" behaviors do you use now?

Pouting	Blaming another	Pushing
Playing sick	Acting helpless	Being shy
Shouting	Maintaining silence	Swearing
Driving discourteously	Quoting facts	Crying
Whining	Nagging	Criticizing
Interrupting	Complaining	Sulking

Demand messages often begin with "you" or imply "you" in the statement. Some demand statements put everything into one general "always" or "never" category. Often a demand message adds an "or else" threat. Try completing these examples.

You always _____.

You must _____.

You never _____.

You are not _____.

You don't _____.

You are _____.

In the long run, demand messages also hurt the demander because they drive others away, leaving the demander lonely and frustrated. Making more demands or changing to a different form of demand only increases the demander's isolation.

Some demand messages I
sometimes give to my spouse: _____.

Some demand messages I don't
like to receive from my spouse: _____.

Ways that demand messages affect me: _____.

Ways that my demand messages affect others: _____.

Defer means that you give in to your spouse and permit demands on you that are not beneficial to you or your spouse.

In some ways defer is the opposite of demand. When you defer, you put yourself down because you see your spouse as more powerful or desirable than you are.

Fearing to lose your partner, you seek to placate or please the other person. As a result, you lose, and your spouse seems to win. However, in the long run both lose.

Here are some typical deferring behaviors that you might use to avoid conflict. Which of these surrender behaviors do you use now?

Being quiet	Nodding "yes, yes"	Being afraid to talk
Speaking only when asked	Accepting blame	Never disagreeing
Carrying a white flag	Being meek and mild	Self-blaming
Avoiding conflict	Feeling ashamed	Usually giving in

Here are some defer statements and actions. Check yourself as you complete them.

You are right about _____.

As usual it's my fault concerning _____.

Whatever you say is _____.

If you say so, then _____.

The defer position often fits well with a demanding spouse. When the deferring spouse becomes more confident and moves to the declare position, the demanding spouse is often puzzled, threatened, or angry about losing the "majority vote" control in the marriage.

Some defer messages I
sometimes give to my spouse: _____.

Some defer messages I don't
like to receive from my spouse: _____.

Ways that defer messages affect me: _____.

Ways that my defer messages affect others: _____.

Detach means that you refuse to work on the conflict or disagreement. No solution is really made to the conflict, so it will probably reappear again at a later time.

Detaching is retreating from each other. When you move away from your partner, you devalue yourself and your spouse. Because you lose contact, you feel lonely, isolated, and abandoned. Both you and your spouse lose.

Here are some typical detaching behaviors that you might use to avoid conflict. Which of these withdrawal behaviors do you use now?

Leaving the room	Working on hobbies	Watching TV
Retreating into silence	Having no time together	Having affairs
Being a workaholic	Avoiding schedules	Hiding
Going home to parent	Leaving spouse out	Becoming depressed
Sleeping in separate beds	Eating alone	Gaining weight
Becoming overinvolved with kids	Taking separate vacations	Disconnecting
Being late	Not answering spouse	Disappearing

Some ways the detach position appears are in these statements. How many of these statements appear in your marriage?

I don't know _____.

Some other time _____.

I'm going out with _____.

I'm too busy to _____.

The detach position is often in response to being rejected and hurt. As a detaching partner you are probably fleeing from something, so you put enough distance between yourself and that threat to make it safe for you.

Some detach messages
I sometimes give to my spouse: _____.

Some detach messages I don't
like to receive from my spouse: _____.

Ways that detach messages affect me: _____.

Ways that my detach messages affect others: _____.

It is lonely for me when _____.

As seen from your viewpoint, how much of each position do you use in coping with conflict? Rank each position and add comments to assist you and your spouse to move more to mutual declare viewpoints.

SIMILAR OR DIFFERENT?

You can reduce some conflict by identifying some of the differences between you and your spouse. Conflict arises because of dissimilarities between you and your partner. They may be different goals, values, styles, background, or interests.

If you respect and value your spouse, you can accept differences as opportunities to learn and to be special individuals. If differences become a problem for you, you can apply your problem-solving skills to resolve the conflict.

You will gain more from this exercise if you make a copy of this page and ask your spouse to do the ratings independently. After you do your ratings, discuss them together.

Use the following letters to identify each response on this rating scale:

M = Man rating himself   H = Woman rating man
F = Woman rating herself   W = Man rating woman

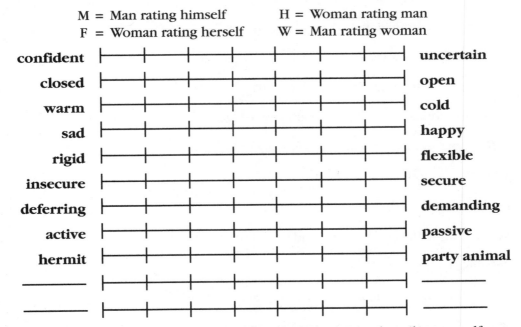

confident	uncertain
closed	open
warm	cold
sad	happy
rigid	flexible
insecure	secure
deferring	demanding
active	passive
hermit	party animal

In the blanks, add other words or phrases that help you to describe yourself more accurately.

In your marriage each person's uniqueness can expand your love power. Differences can be refreshing since they expand the opportunities for both partners to grow and learn.

Areas where we agree are _____.

Areas where we differ yet value each other are _____.

WHICH ACTIONS TURN CONFLICTS INTO POSITIVES FOR YOU?

Here are some ways that couples can turn conflicts into constructive patterns. Working together to increase positives enables you to feel closer, loved, and more competent with each other.

How It Works for Me	Doesn't Work	Helps Some	Helps a Lot
Being clear about what each spouse is to do	_____	_____	_____
Agreeing on who will make specific decisions	_____	_____	_____
Spouses sharing power and choices	_____	_____	_____
One spouse making most of the decisions	_____	_____	_____
Seeing differences as part of a healthy marriage	_____	_____	_____
Resolving every conflict before doing anything else	_____	_____	_____
Allowing room to express anger	_____	_____	_____
Talking with relatives about our conflicts	_____	_____	_____
Negotiating with each other to find useful solutions	_____	_____	_____
Deciding whether the conflict is worth the battle	_____	_____	_____
Behind the anger, finding the threat to me or spouse	_____	_____	_____
Being able to hear each other express views without interrupting	_____	_____	_____

CONFLICT RESOLUTION ATTITUDES

Conflict occurs because the wants and expectations of each person involved cannot all be achieved. There are two basic possibilities in every conflict:

1. I will get my way regardless of what happens to my spouse or others involved.

2. We will modify our objectives so that the results can benefit all who are involved.

DISAGREEMENTS ARE TO BE EXPECTED

No two people can agree on everything all of the time. Conflicts and disagreements are part of the daily lives of couples. The important question is, How do you and your partner handle disagreements and conflicts?

P **L O V E** **W** **E** **R**	*If two of you agree on earth concerning anything that they ask, it will be done for them by My Father in heaven. For where two or three are gathered together in My name, I am there in the midst of them (Matt. 18:19–20).*

NOURISHING LOVE POWER IN YOUR MARRIAGE

Enriching your marriage for golden harvests

You and your spouse have explored the four major dimensions of love power and how your communication connects your future, your positives, your resources, and your negatives.

In Part 7, you can incorporate these basics into your marital journey across your lifetimes. You will begin with growth opportunities that you and your spouse can initiate on your own. Marriage enrichment expands your couple support networks. There are also guides to finding professional help when you need it.

Chapter 36

Growth Opportunities

"There are so many good possibilities for us," commented Ken as he reached for his coffee. "As soon as we get around to it, we'll do more fun things."

"I agree, and there is a way," Barb replied as she reached for a round disk on the table. Holding it out to Ken, she continued, "Here is our TOIT."

"Our TOIT?" asked Ken. "What's that?"

Smiling, Barb explained, "You said we could have more fun as soon as we get around to it, so here is our round TOIT. Are you ready?"

"Ready! Let's begin right now," Ken answered as he pulled Barb into a playful bear hug and began covering her with kisses.

There are many "round to it" opportunities for you and your spouse to continue to grow in your power to love. As you read about some of them, mark the ones you are using and want to expand, then create others for your marriage journey.

MILEPOSTS AND TURNING POINTS

In your marriage journey you have many once-in-a-lifetime turning points. Many of these marriage markers are major events, such as your big promotion at work, a move to a new home, birth of a child, and deaths of loved ones. Others may be less critical, such as getting your first gray hair.

You may record some of these mileposts with snapshots, videotape, canceled checks, letters, and notes in a journal or diary. You may wish you had a record of others as you look back over your journey. You may discover that some changes were much more important than you realized at the time while others that seemed so critical turned out to make little difference.

Mileposts that brought us happiness: _____.

Mileposts that mark disappointments: _____.

Ways I want to remember our turning points: _____.

> **P**
> **L O V E**
> **W**
> **E**
> **R**
>
> *Meanings are not so much in what happens to you but in how you accept and respond to events.*

FUN TIMES AND ACTIVITIES

What do you do for fun? What have you and your spouse done just for fun in the past several days?

Activities we do for fun are _____.

Some quieter fun times are _____.

Important sources of joy are _____.

Our next fun time will be _____.

> **P**
> **L O V E**
> **W**
> **E**
> **R**
>
> *Seek the LORD and His strength; Seek His face evermore! (1 Chron. 16:11).*

CELEBRATING YOUR FAITH

Your church offers many opportunities to join with others in celebrating your faith in God's love to the world.

Prayer reminds us that we are not alone in this world, even for one day of our lives. We need only to ask God for help and guidance in our lives and in everything we do and say. Through study and prayer we become aware of others' crying, praising, and praying and are renewed so we will be able to help those around us, no matter where we are.

My prayer for guidance includes _____.

I ask for awakening my spirit and clearing my sight for _____.

I pray my life will be filled with _____.

Help us to give praise for _____.

Support us to work to accomplish the Lord's will in _____.

Make us instruments for healing of _____.

Since this is the day the Lord has made, guide us to _____.

NETWORKS

Through friendship networks, you and your spouse have many opportunities to grow. As you explored earlier, friendships with other couples give you new perspectives and support you in both good and bad times. You also encourage the couples, perhaps much more than you know.

My informal friendship groups are _____.

The group my spouse and I enjoy most is _____.

Community groups in which we participate are _____.

MARRIAGE IN THE MEDIA

Through movies, television, drama, books, and magazines, you can observe both successful and unsuccessful marriages. In any drama involving marriage and family situations you can observe the values of the characters, the impacts that each character wants to make on the others, and what actually happens.

Drama in any form provides at least three levels or views in relation to its impact on your marriage.

First, as an uninvolved observer, you watch what is happening between the characters. You can trace couple patterns and consider how the characters might have acted to achieve alternate outcomes.

Second, become aware of the impact of the drama on you. What happens to you as a result of watching the drama? Are you more confident, more anxious, pleased, or disappointed?

Third, with this new information how will you and your spouse change your interactions? From media you can become aware of positive skills that make marriage and family life succeed. You also become aware of negative patterns that disrupt and destroy marriages and the lives of others around the couples.

A drama (play, story) that is important for us: _____.

What happened between the characters (the plot): _____.

Impacts of the drama on me and my spouse: _____.

How my spouse and I have changed as a result: _____.

MEMORY MARKERS

Memories are markers along your life and marriage journeys. They enable you to see the power you have to overcome difficulties and give you confidence for your future. Skills and habits depend upon accurately remembering the past so you can use it in the next stages of your journeys.

Here is a way to explore and celebrate some significant markers. For each category, write a word or phrase to name the event and your reactions to it. Then take some time to share your findings with your spouse.

	Event	*My Feelings About It*
A very happy occasion	_____	_____
A time when you succeeded	_____	_____
The biggest surprise you ever had	_____	_____
The time you were most angry	_____	_____

	Event	*My Feelings About It*
The thing you always feared most	_____	_____
Your most secret wish	_____	_____
A time you felt most loved and accepted	_____	_____
A recurring dream	_____	_____

P
L O V E
W
E
R

I want to be the spouse you dream I will be, so I love and accept you just as you are since I know that love can free us to become the persons God calls us to be.

YOUR PLAN FOR POSITIVE CHANGES

Together, select an example of a specific change that you would like to make in your relationship as a couple. Then make a plan that will help each of you to make this change. These steps can aid you in creating your plan.

Describe the situation and topic to work on.

_____

What does each want to happen in this situation (goals)?

_____

What could each do to accomplish the goals?

_____

What will you actually do to reach the goal you want?

_____

How will you know when you reach the goal? How do the results match the goal you set?

_____

How will you share feedback with each other about how the plan is working? How does each feel about the outcome?

_____

Chapter 37

Marriage Enrichment Programs

"We just registered for the marriage enrichment retreat next month," the Wrights announced. "This is our third weekend since we married."

"What's that?" asked the Ventures.

"It's a fun-filled, fact-packed recharge for your love batteries," teased the Wrights. "How about coming with us?"

"Maybe you could tell us more about it so we can make it a Wright Venture," replied the Ventures.

Since the beginnings of civilization, most nations and religions have recognized the vital contributions that strong, stable marriage and family systems make to all of society. Both church and state have tried to support marriage since it is the central bond that holds a family together.

Among many models for marriage are three biblical examples. The Song of Solomon describes the wholesome joy and pleasure that marriage closeness and intimacy can provide. In Proverbs 31 is a description of a woman who excels at being a wife, mother, merchant, and sage. In 1 Timothy 3, the highest church leaders (bishops) were to be married only once; they were to be good husbands and fathers, temperate, sensible, not a drunkard or violent or quarrelsome, and able to manage well.

There are many good marriage models, but often they are not known to the couples who most need them. Although at various times in the past churches provided some teaching and models for marriage, most couples learned how to live in marriage by observing their relatives and friends and by trial and error.

Some good marriage models for us are _____.

We use these insights in our marriage in these ways: _____.

PURPOSES OF MARRIAGE ENRICHMENT

The general purpose of marriage enrichment programs is to strengthen marriage and family life. The primary way this is done is through couples' groups. In addition, some enrichment programs publish magazines and other resources for couples, train retreat leaders, and set quality standards for events. Various marriage enrichment groups cooperate to sponsor conferences and try to affect legislation and media in favor of good marriage and family life.

Some marriage enrichment organizations seek to improve community services that help couples and families be more successful. In these and other ways marriage enrichment tries to educate the public about positive marriage and family models. Many leaders in the marriage enrichment field are also ministers and professional therapists with careers that include services to couples and families.

Marriage enrichment has also been extended to engaged couples and other couples who are planning to marry. Some programs especially try to serve specific types of couples or topics.

P	*Let me see your face,*
L O V E	*Let me hear your voice;*
W	*For your voice is sweet,*
E	*And your face is lovely. . . .*
R	*Set me as a seal upon your heart, . . .*
	For love is as strong as death. . . .
	Many waters cannot quench love,
	Nor can the floods drown it
	(Song of Sol. 2:14; 8:6–7).

SOME WELL-KNOWN MARRIAGE ENRICHMENT PROGRAMS

Here is a sample of marriage enrichment programs.

ACME: The Association of Couples for Marriage Enrichment trains and certifies marriage enrichment leader couples and publishes listings of upcoming marriage enrichment events. The format emphasizes modeling by leader couples, couple skill training, and enjoyable fellowship activities for couples. Events emphasize personal, emotional, spiritual, and skill development for husbands and wives as individuals and as couples.

Marriage Encounter has many Catholic and Protestant denominational expressions in many countries around the world. With a strong emphasis on spiritual development, the format includes presentations to which couples write responses they can later discuss privately. *Engaged Encounter* has been adapted for couples preparing for marriage.

ACME and *Marriage Encounter* jointly publish *Marriage*, a monthly magazine that contains many useful articles, quotes, and announcements with practical tips on improving your marriage.

Interpersonal Communications Programs, founded by Sherod Miller, train professional persons in one-day workshops to use several basic communication tools such as the "Awareness Wheel" and problem-solving techniques. These leaders then offer couples workshops in weekend and weekly formats.

Relationship Enhancement, developed by Bernard Guerney, emphasizes specific skill training for couples. Events use a combination of presentations, skill practice with feedback, and homework to enable couples to accomplish goals.

Getting the Love You Want, developed by Harville Hendrix, is a Saturday morning to Sunday evening workshop for couples. In these intensive workshops couples connect current patterns to unfulfilled childhood hurts and losses and learn marriage communication and problem-solving skills.

PREP has been developed by Howard Markman and his colleagues for couples who are preparing for marriage. Usually offered in five sessions of three hours each, the program provides information about many aspects of couple communication and emotional functioning.

Couples who talk together every day never become strangers. Ten-second hugs are better than two-second curses. Love enriches both the giver and the receiver. Be crazy with love and surprised by joy and mystery.

Christian PREP, adapted from *PREP* by Scott Stanley, a colleague of Howard Markman, undergirds the *PREP* program with an evangelical Christian framework that includes spiritual development for couples.

Recovery of Hope is a program that offers a Saturday morning format for troubled couples who are trying to decide what to do about their marriages. A week-long intensive program is also available in some locations. *Recovery of Hope* is offered through the Mennonite hospital system and other centers.

Growing Together is a couples' program built around the *Prepare/Enrich* couple inventories. Usually meeting for eight sessions, couples use inventory results to guide them in exploring, understanding, and deciding directions for their relationship.

Denominational Marriage Enrichment Programs are offered by many of the larger Christian denominations and independent church groups and agencies. With a variety of formats and content, these programs are usually designed and offered by trained ministers and laypersons within each religious group.

Christian Marriage Enrichment is offered in a variety of formats by H. Norman Wright.

Chapter 38

Professional Help

On their commute home Mike and Tom were swapping stories, complaining about traffic, and sharing opinions. After a pause, Mike began, "You know that Mary and I have been having some rough times recently. Well, we finally decided to do something about it. Maybe you know where we can find some help."

"What kind of help?" Tom asked, encouraging with a bit of humor. "Lawyer, therapist, plumber, or what?"

"We are going to try to make our marriage work, so I don't think we need an attorney. The plumbing is okay, so I guess we are looking for a marriage counselor type." Mike continued, "Know anyone?"

"Maybe," Tom responded. "There's a psychologist in our church couples' group, and I know our pastor has contact with several family professionals."

"That's a start," Mike said. "What's our next step?"

WHAT KINDS OF PROFESSIONAL HELP?

Therapy and *counseling* overlap so much that the words are often used interchangeably. Professional counseling and therapy refer to procedures that help you become aware of sources of your conflict, develop options, make choices, and take appropriate charge of your life.

How this is done varies somewhat across therapists and disciplines, yet there is far more similarity than difference between good therapists.

My understanding of therapy and counseling is _____.

My feelings about getting professional help are _____.

It is desirable to have a medical checkup as part of therapy because of the complicated relationship between body, mind, and spirit. A good medical evaluation can identify whether biochemical factors, medication side effects, hormone imbalances, and other physical factors may be contributing to what seems to be psychological and marital distress.

WHICH TYPE OF THERAPY?

Since therapy is such a personal matter, you must feel confident of your therapist's training, skills, attitudes, personal qualities, and faith assumptions. In selecting a therapist, you may want to interview two or three (probably paying the standard fee) before you decide with whom to work. If you have friends who had good success with a therapist, their suggestions may assist you in your search. Even so, a therapist who works well with a friend is not necessarily right for you.

Qualities I want in a therapist are _____.

These qualities would help me and
my spouse in these ways: _____.

In selecting a therapist, ask questions about training, treatment approaches, fees, treatment length and options, and other matters related to your situation. If you encounter a therapist who does not want you to ask questions, that may be a warning not to continue with the person.

Marriage and family therapy is available from psychologists, marriage and family counselors, pastoral counselors, professional counselors, social workers, and psychiatrists. Depending on your state, other titles may also appear.

Christian persons are at work in each of these professions. Some may label themselves as Christian counselors or biblical counselors. Other equally dedicated therapists integrate Christian faith with their professional practice and are willing to discuss faith issues as they appear in counseling. There are several valid ways to use faith, prayer, the Bible, and other religious resources in counseling. A competent therapist will be open to discussing these approaches with you at your request.

```
P
L O V E       The wisdom that is from above is first
W             pure, then peaceable, gentle, willing to
E             yield, full of mercy and good fruits (James
R             3:17).
```

REASONS COUPLES DON'T SEEK HELP

Listed are some reasons that couples may not seek help when they are in trouble. Check the three or four primary reasons couples would be reluctant to seek marital help. How would you overcome each hindrance to get the help you need?

_____ 1. One or both partners are embarrassed to admit failure.

_____ 2. One or both partners don't want to change.

_____ 3. They think things can't be improved.

_____ 4. Relatives or friends would be offended.

_____ 5. They will not use money to buy resources.

_____ 6. One spouse thinks the other will not change.

_____ 7. The couple does not know about marriage resources.

_____ 8. Partners are not committed to each other.

_____ 9. Partners may not know that they are hurting others.

_____ 10. Partners have little hope for change.

_____ 11. Other: _____

IF ONE NEEDS HELP, BOTH NEED HELP

Any of the negative conditions discussed in Part 5 probably indicate a need for therapy. Since your marriage is a system consisting of you and your spouse plus influences from relatives, friends, and other sources, it is never a question of which spouse or whether only one spouse needs therapy. Both need to do therapeutic work to improve the situation. Even if a problem seems to appear in one spouse only, you can be sure that both spouses contributed to the situation.

Nevertheless, if your spouse will not go to therapy with you, go by yourself. Your improvement may make it safer for your spouse to begin therapy and make changes because you are becoming more caring, sensitive, warm, and open to growth.

YOU KNOW YOU NEED HELP WHEN . . .

Here are some signs that professional help may be needed.

You work on a problem, and it still doesn't improve: _____.

You feel depressed, full of rage, or out of control: _____.

You keep withdrawing from each other: _____.

You are sure everything is your spouse's fault: _____.

Unexplained changes in mood,
appearance, and personal habits occur: _____.

You or your spouse moves out of the home: _____.

You and your spouse rigidly oppose each other
concerning values, parenting, relatives, or other issues: _____.

You don't know what help you need or where to find it: _____.

If you or your spouse think one or both of you need help, try finding the appropriate help together. If one refuses, the other still needs to find help without the spouse. Begin your search by consulting with your pastor, physician, or trusted friend. If that doesn't produce what you need, consult with a therapist. Most therapists and counseling agencies are available for one session consultation to help you make decisions about the type of assistance you need.

Part 8

REACHING OUT TO FAMILIES AND OTHER COUPLES

Sharing your caring with children and other neighbors

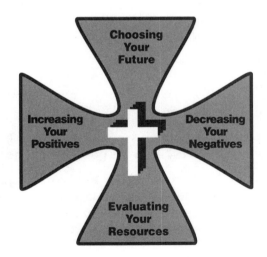

God created you, calls you to love, and gives you power to become His child. Spiritual formation is the forming of your spirit that permeates your life and makes you a whole person before God, open to understanding yourself and learning how to reach out to others in love. Spiritual formation is reaching upward to God, inward to yourself, and outward to others. All three dimensions are equally important.

Reaching upward to God means _____.

Reaching inward to myself means _____.

Reaching outward to others means _____.

These three dimensions of spiritual formation reflect Jesus' great commandment to love God and love your neighbor as yourself (Matt. 22:36–40): (1) As you walk with God, you learn about yourself and your neighbor; (2) as you understand yourself more, you become transformed by the Holy Spirit and understand God and others; and (3) as you seek to love and care for your neighbor (spouse, children, family, friends, colleagues, and others in the world), you know God better and discover the potentials in yourself. Each dimension informs the other two, constantly blending spiritual formation into your life journey. That is why love power is so basic to marriage and to all of life.

Marriage is important because this special man-woman relationship is God's way of giving you a laboratory to learn to love. Marriage is also important because the husband-as-father and wife-as-mother shape and socialize their children as citizens and as children of God's kingdom of love and power. In this sense each family affects us all, for better or worse, just as society (all of us) influences each family and marriage.

How our marriage affects our parenting: _____.

Ways our family affects others: _____.

How God works for good in these ways : _____.

In the previous parts of this workbook you have explored how love power permeates your future, your resources, and your positives and negatives as a couple.

The chapters in Part 8 are brief introductions to major expansions of love power beyond your marriage to your children, to other couples, and to society and the world. You are invited to consider how your spiritual formation is expressed in each area.

(You may want to write a statement that expresses your commitment to apply the love power principles in your lives. On the next page is a certificate you can use to put your commitment in writing. Use it, or create your own statement.)

CHRISTIAN COMMITMENT CERTIFICATE

Every day God gives us a new day in our life journey.

Because I am thankful to God for love, power, and grace to be the best person possible,

I, _____, commit myself to

God for _____

_____,

my spouse for _____

_____,

our child for _____

_____,

my family for _____

_____,

and others for _____

_____

_____.

P
L O V E
O
W
E
R

Stir up the gift of God which is in you. . . . For God has not given us a spirit of fear, but of power and of love and of a sound mind (2 Tim. 1:6–7).

Chapter 39

Parenting with Love Power in Families

"Parenting children is another way that you learn how God parents us."

"Figure out the type of person you want your child to be and then be that person."

"As a parent, never make a rule you cannot enforce."

"Children need love, structure, freedom, and values."

"Children cannot grow in shade that smothers."

"The good and bad in society begin in the homes of the nation."

"By talking with your child each day, you will never become strangers."

"Don't take parenting seriously, but always take your child seriously."

"The way you treat your child is the way that your child will later treat you."

"All the rules are summed up in the commandment: Love God and love your neighbor as yourself."

These are a few guides for parenting children. You probably have heard many more. What are some of your guides for parenting?

An important parenting guide is _____.

How did you obtain this guide? _____

A guide I do not like is _____.

Reasons I dislike this rule are _____.

For couples who are parents, this chapter is a very brief overview of how love power applies to parenting. It invites you and your spouse to review the love power principles we have discussed for your marriage and apply them to parenting your child. If you do not have a child, you may skip this chapter or use it to find ways you can encourage other parents.

SPOUSE COMMITMENT, SUPPORT, AND COOPERATION AS PARENTS

The four basic love power dimensions of future, resources, positives, and negatives are connected through your communication in many ways.

Like marriage, parenting also begins with the choices you make about the future for your child and yourselves. You choose to commit yourselves to values that become the basis for deciding which resources you use and for evaluating skills, events, patterns, and situations as positive or negative.

Important values we hold as parents are _____.

In marriage you commit yourselves to God and to each other as spouses. Your marriage commitment is basic to your parenting because it is the center around which you set boundaries and organize your parenting commitments and patterns.

When your marriage is healthy and you respect and trust each other as spouses, you are able to talk about any parenting concern. When your personal needs are being met in marriage and other ways, you free your child to grow and develop.

P
L O V E   *As many as received Him, to them He gave*
W   *the right to become children of God (John*
E   *1:12).*
R

YOUR PARENTING MANUAL

With nearly everything you get an instruction manual. With a newborn baby, however, the hospital gives you the baby and sends you home with no instruction manual. In a sense you have instructions for parenting from your childhood experiences and from your discussions with your spouse and others.

Instructions I would like are _____.

I would like more help and information about _____.

Some ways I (we) could help other parents are _____.

LEARNING AND PARENTING

Every child learns the patterns and habits that form character and personality. When your child does something you do not approve or fails to do something you want, a very difficult question is, "How did you teach your child to do that?" You likely will respond that you did not teach that. In one sense, you are correct, but at deeper levels in ways you may not have noticed, you have modeled patterns for your child and rewarded your child in ways you may not have intended.

A pattern our child follows: _____.

Ways our child learned it: _____.

My part in it: _____.

Parenting involves guiding children toward better goals and helping them to improve their resources and skills for reaching their desired goals. Changing a child's behavior involves changing the reward or the goal or the child's resources. This is relatively simple while your child is very young, but it becomes increasingly complex as your child grows older. Reaching the goal is the reward.

A good habit of our child: _____.

The goal this habit tries to achieve: _____.

How the results reward the child: _____.

How this encourages the child to repeat the habit: _____.

A bad or hurtful habit of our child: _____.

The real goal this habit tries to achieve: _____.

How the results keep the habit going: _____.

How this encourages the child to repeat the habit: _____.

How we can change the goal or
reward to create a replacement habit: _____.

You and your spouse are the key persons in your child's learning. Increasingly along the way you bring others, such as teachers, friends, and coaches, into this process to assist in this nurture.

CONSISTENCY: THE FOUNDATION FOR PARENTING

Your child needs a consistent, stable environment. As parents, you create safe, secure, dependable home and family structures when what you say and what you do match. Your child can always count on you and your spouse for love and care. Your child can count on you, which creates in your child a sense of predictability and dependability.

You create consistency when you have regular times for meals and rules are fair and apply to all in the family. Changes can be made only when all who are affected by the rule are involved in making the change. Consistency means you care enough to stick with your vows and goals, just as God sticks with the world, even when it might be easier to abandon it. In many ways you provide emotional and spiritual security for your child.

A consistent pattern that is important: _____.

How I feel about being consistent: _____.

How my spouse feels about being consistent: _____.

When things are not dependable or stable, a child becomes fearful and anxious. The child comes to mistrust others because what seems true now may not be true tomorrow.

OPENNESS TO YOUR GROWING CHILD

Openness and flexibility come out of a consistent, secure family structure. Like a well-rooted tree, a secure family enables you and your child to be open to learning new skills and patterns and to grow in love.

What can you learn from your child? You probably will learn more about God's world from your child than your child learns from you.

Some insights I have received from my child: _____.

Ways I try to be open to listening to my child: _____.

When you and your spouse are open to each other, you can be open to your child by respecting your child's viewpoints. Even when you disagree, you can affirm your child for thinking and becoming independent.

Imagine your child as a child of God, as a full member of your family, and as a citizen of your community and nation. Your child can tell you when something hurts, when things are unfair and might be different, and when things are going right. Sometimes a child will be more honest than adults, but adults may try to silence this honesty and truth.

Only as you learn about your child's expanding sense of self and the world can you adapt your knowledge to fit the growing edges of your child's developing self. This liberates your child to be different from you, yet respect you as a trustworthy guide to life.

Ways I encourage my child to be
honest and trustworthy: _____.

Ways I show appreciation to my child: _____.

Adjustments we have made in family
rules because of feedback from our child: _____.

KNOWLEDGE OF CHILD AND ADOLESCENT DEVELOPMENT

Because of your love power, you want to learn what to expect at each age and stage of your child's development. Then you can set realistic expectations that encourage confident growth without overwhelming or discouraging your child or you.

Some dependable sources of
knowledge about child development: _____.

Persons with whom I talk about
details of child development: _____.

RESOURCES IN CHURCH, SCHOOL, AND COMMUNITY

Since children learn so much from people around them, you need to help your child associate with others who have basic values and attitudes with which you agree. You will often find these groups in your church, in child care settings, with some neighbors (but probably not others), and with some relatives and friends.

Parenting classes, school-related associations, community recreation and sports groups, and other groups usually attract families with similar values and goals. Although you will not agree with everything any group does, you probably will have enough in common to feel comfortable in discussing your parenting concerns and in encouraging your child to participate in the activities.

Classes that I have attended are _____.

Ways I distinguish between core
values to keep and passing fads are _____.

FAMILY STRUCTURES AND PARENTING SITUATIONS

The classic family structure is a father, a mother, and their own biological children who live together as a family from the children's births through their growing up and leaving home and later coming back to visit with their children, your grandchildren.

This description fits only a minority of families today. Many families are blended together with children from previous marriages. In addition some couples adopt children who may come into the home at different ages.

Our family situation is _____.

My feelings about our situation are _____.

Blended families usually involve some type of child custody arrangement that affects the parenting authority of all involved. Children of divorce must often deal with living with one biological parent and visiting the other biological parent who may have different rules and expectations.

With divorce, the child must also adjust to the remarriage of one or both biological parents, which brings stepparents into the picture and ends whatever hopes the child may have held that the biological parents would reunite. Normal sibling conflicts may be amplified when a new stepparent brings children into the child's original home.

Concerning a child from a
previous marriage, I feel _____.

Concerning a child from a
previous marriage, my spouse feels _____.

This affects our marriage and
parenting patterns now by _____.

In the context of God's love, love power enables you and your spouse to care for each child, regardless of biological, adoptive, or other relationship. The four dimensions of love power apply to any parenting situation.

THE END OF PARENTING

Every parent at times may feel exhausted or frustrated and wonder whether parenting will ever end. It does! Parenting is not a lifetime job. Your job as a parent ends when your child can take a place in society as a mature, independent adult. If you gradually pass control of your child's life to your child, you increasingly become a friend as adult to adult.

How I feel about parenting: _____.

How my spouse feels about parenting: _____.

Times when I feel parenting will never end: _____.

Times when it seems as if parenting goes too fast: _____.

One of the finest gifts you can give your child is keeping your marriage healthy and successful.

You begin to prepare for your child to leave home when your child is born. Birth itself is God's appointed way to push your infant out into the world. Parenting is continuing to prepare your child to become a citizen of the world and a child of God in the same ways you enjoy God's grace, love, and friendship.

How we are preparing our child to leave home: _____.

How we feel about our child growing up: _____.

Some advantages of an empty nest: _____.

ON TO A NEW BEGINNING AS GRANDPARENTS

If your child has children, you enter the enjoyable grandparent relationship with them. Even if you are not an "official" grandparent, you have many opportunities to be substitute grandparents to other children.

Grandparents provide living links to past heritage and perspectives on parenting and the world that enable children to compare situations and clarify their value and faith.

Think of your grandparents as you answer these statements.

The grandparents I had most contact with were _____.

As a child, my experience with grandparents was _____.

Hobbies and other interests my grandparents shared are _____.

A favorite activity I did with
my grandparents was _____.

When I remember this, I feel _____.

The best times I spent with my grandparents were _____.

I felt important and valued around my _____.

For parents unable to take their children to visit their grandparents who may live a distance away, a grandparents' day or camp or other contact between children and the senior generation could be helpful. Some older citizens can help provide child care and share skills with children of all ages.

Children enjoy stories, and grandparents usually have many good stories to tell. Younger children may be surprised to discover that their parents were once kids, also, and older children and adolescents may discover personal views of history that are not easily available in books. Grandparents can give gifts of encouragement and good memories to grandchildren as they share genuine unconditional love with each grandchild.

Adopting a grandparent or grandchild
could be rewarding in these ways: _____.

Our church could start a grandparents-
and-grandchildren-day or activity by _____.

By living love power in your marriage, you provide a positive, healthy model of love for your child and encourage each other in the challenging and rewarding task of launching a child into the world of the future.

Chapter 40

Couples Enriching Couples

As you grow through love power in your own marriage, the world needs you and your partner as modern Samaritans to be a mentor couple to other couples. Consider this adaptation of Jesus' parable of the good Samaritan (Luke 10:30–36).

Betty and Bill fell in love, married, and began their journey toward living happily ever after. Along the way, however, they found that they often disagreed on which fork in the road to take and how to arrange their lives together. Compare their interpretations of their journey.

Betty's view: "Bill became more and more involved in his work. He withdrew from me, never did anything I asked, and spent a lot of time away from home with his friends. Sometimes we would get into fights, so we just stayed away from each other. At least it was safer that way. Our marriage took on a thick protective wall of coldness and bitterness.

"I didn't know what to do, so we decided to have a baby to save our marriage. Now I know that job was too big for any baby! For a while the early romance of marriage seemed to return in the fun of sex, but after I became pregnant, the old control and abandonment feelings came back even more. Things became more difficult, so by the time the baby arrived, we had our final divorce papers. It looks like we have passed the diseases of love from our parents to their grandchild. So now I have a child but no husband. What a sad legacy."

Bill's view: "Betty became preoccupied with the children. We rarely went out together or had sex. She was always finding fault with everything I did. That's probably because she listened too much to her mother. At first our disagreements seemed minor, but they grew into major conflicts. I wanted Betty to respond to me, but she didn't. No matter what I did, she misinterpreted it as something bad. The love we had vanished, leaving just one storm after another of anger and pain.

"We tried to turn to our families for help, but my parents had divorced years ago and Betty's parents were in the middle of a divorce. My sister's marriage is a worse mess than ours, and Betty's two brothers are both divorced. The couple we thought were doing okay just said, 'Yeah, we know what you mean. If you find any answers, tell us. We need them, too.' "

Do you know couples like Bill and Betty? _____

In what ways can you help them
recover hope and love in their marriages? _____

MENTOR COUPLES CAN HELP

What a difference a mentor couple could have made in Betty and Bill's married life. In addition, if someone had been able to help their parents to be more successful in their marriages, how different Betty and Bill would have been when they married each other.

Most couples who need help in their marriages are not likely to seek help. As you saw in Part 7, there are many reasons that couples are reluctant to seek help from others, whether friends or professional therapists. When couples are in trouble, they are in pain, their children and relatives are hurting, and neighborhoods, schools, businesses, and all of society are damaged.

Many excellent resources are available to these couples, and in every community many healthy couples could be the living links between couples in difficulties and resources they need.

Some potential mentor couples I know are _____.

Some couples who might appreciate mentor help are _____.

These couples could cooperate
for better marriages in these ways: _____.

P
L O V E
W
E
R

Mentor couples are living links between available resources and couples who need them.

HOW TO BE A MENTOR COUPLE

Mentor couples can reach out as friends to other couples. As friends, they can speak directly to the couple and enable them to move beyond the fears and uncertainties that block them from getting the help they need. How can you do this?

First, you decide that you want to reach out to other couples in friendship.

Second, you now know the major love power dimensions of marriage, and you are practicing them in your marriage. In these ways you check how well you are doing as a couple so that you identify the strengths you have to share.

Third, you can create ways to provide information about resources to couples who want or need them. You may do this informally through friendship networks. In addition, you may organize to reach out to others.

How I feel about reaching out to other couples: _____.

Some marriage perspectives we could share: _____.

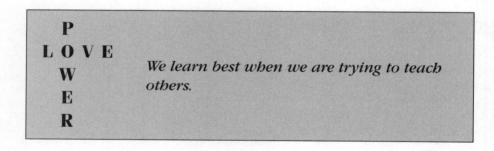

P
L O V E
O
W
E
R

We learn best when we are trying to teach others.

WAYS TO OPEN CONVERSATIONS WITH COUPLES

As a mentor couple, you and your spouse may meet with the other couple several times, or you may see one or both of the partners in informal ways. You may visit as couples with all four persons present. Sometimes the two wives or two husbands may meet separately.

As you talk with the other couple, your initial goal is to discover their vision or guidelines for their marriage and how each spouse lives them. As you observe the couple in action, try to become aware of their deeper strengths and note their areas of needed growth. You can use your experiences to connect to couples as you share how you and your spouse coped with similar issues and problems.

The advantage of seeing both spouses together is that you can observe how they interact with each other as well as hear their comments to your questions. With both partners, you can note who does most of the talking, who is really controlling the relationship, which communication channels and patterns they use, and which topics seem to be difficult or pleasant for them.

These suggested questions and topics follow the love power dimensions. You can rearrange, modify, and add your own topics and questions.

Journey

What is the couple's situation?
Where are they on their life and marriage journey? _____
(*Consider age, educational status, occupation, type of relationship, and family situation.*)

Future

What are goals and expectations
of each spouse for self? _____

What are goals and expectations for the spouse? _____

How is each spouse committed to the marriage? _____

What faith commitments undergird their marriage? _____

Where does each spouse want to
be in five or ten years from now? _____

Which images, visions, and principles
for marriage guide each partner? _____

Sources of these images and guides are _____.

Resources

How does the family background of each
spouse influence the marriage now? _____

How do the personality and temperament
of each spouse affect the marriage? _____

What support groups and networks
does the couple have or need? _____

How can you connect them to help that need? _____

P
L O V E   *Our need for God's love is endless. Our*
W   *hope for God's world is deep. Our journey*
E   *with God is eternal.*
R

Positives

What are the positive marriage patterns
of these two persons? _____

What have been the most humorous experiences
the partners have had together? _____

What other impressive experiences
have been theirs? _____

How do they affirm and encourage each other? _____

How do they turn difficulties into assets? _____

Negatives

What negative patterns or habits interfere
with their marriage success? _____

What helps does this couple
need to stop these negatives? _____

What helps can you provide? _____

How can you encourage them to
get additional help they may need? _____

Communication

What are the primary ways each
communicates with the other? _____

What problems and crises has the couple faced? _____

How have the partners coped with them? _____

What suggestions for a successful
marriage do these spouses have to offer? _____

What suggestions do they have for improving
their marriage or for educating others for marriage? _____

Add other questions that you develop. In an hour of conversation with a couple, you can discover many important insights about them that will help them and you and your spouse live love power more effectively in your marriages.

P
L O V E   *The Word became flesh and dwelt among*
W   *us, and we beheld His glory, . . . full of*
E   *grace and truth (John 1:14).*
R

Chapter 41

Love Power in Society

"Parents and teachers can join together for family life education that enables us all to be good role models for our children and teens."

"That movie was a great example of what a marriage really can be."

"It's good business for companies to consider the families of their employees. It reduces absenteeism, increases morale and productivity, and shows we are working together for worthwhile goals."

"A person has to be taught to respect self, respect others, and respect property. This respect has to begin in the family."

"We banded together and chased the drug dealers out of our neighborhood."

"We need laws that encourage each family to be the best they can be and free families to make their own choices."

This workbook focuses on marriage because couples are the adults who create and control the home environment for their children and others living with them.

Since you have used this workbook to enhance and enrich your marriage, consider now how you can influence the ways society supports positive marriage and family images, values, and programs. You have resources that can help other couples. You may share your resources informally with friends, through your paid and volunteer work, and through groups that seek to improve society by improving marriage and family relationships.

In these ways you can increase your power to change the world as you encourage couples to make their homes havens of blessing and places of peace.

How I feel about problems in society: _____.

List some problems that now create, or have created, crises in the lives of persons you know (*for example, divorce, alcohol abuse, assault, job loss, housing problems, etc.*): _____ .

Talk with your spouse about how each problem results from couples who have trouble in their marriage and family relationships.

WHICH CRISIS IN THE WORLD?

Choose your crisis. At the root of most crises, in one form or another, is an unsuccessful family in which children were mistreated, or had bad role models, and were not helped to grow up as good citizens. At the center of an unsuccessful family is an unsuccessful couple.

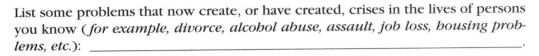

P
L O V E   *I press toward the goal for the prize*
W   *of the upward call of God in Christ Jesus*
E   *(Phil. 3:14).*
R

MEDIA IMAGES OF MARRIAGE

Many contradictory images of marriage and family lifestyles are presented in every type of media. You evaluate these various presentations as you set your personal expectations about marriage and family living. Adapt the questions to fit your interests, and add other questions that you can use to evaluate a specific presentation.

Here are some ways you can become more aware of the positive and negative family images and values in society. You may already be in a career that gives you opportunity to strengthen positive marriages, or you may decide to volunteer time, money, leadership, and energy to improve marriage and family living in some way.

Magazines, Newspapers, and Books

Consider the magazine, newspaper, and book displays in your local stores as well as the resources you read.

Which magazines, newspapers, and books
lift up positive aspects of marriage? _____

What are these messages and images? _____

Which magazines and newspapers try
to sell negative aspects of marriage? _____

What can you and others do to correct them? _____

Movies and Television

Notice current and recent movies and television programs. Dramatic presentations usually have some type of conflict that must be resolved. Some values are emphasized or supported, while other values are rejected in each of these productions. You may analyze the important factors or influences on each character in relation to that person's approach to marriage and family love power values.

What conflicts are presented
in these dramatic situations? _____

How could the conflict have been
avoided or resolved better in real life? _____

What influences do these programs have
on most adults, adolescents, or children? _____

Music

Every type of music contains references to men and women, marriage, and family relationships. Usually, these meanings are carried by the lyrics, although some meanings may be associated with certain musical themes. Some music originated in a dramatic setting such as an opera or a Broadway musical production. Think about some of the music with which you are familiar.

Examples of music that contains
images and values concerning marriage: _____.

How does it encourage or discourage
good marriage and family living? _____

Visual Arts

Paintings, sculpture, architecture, commercial arts, and other visual art forms
sometimes illustrate marriage and family values.

How do these encourage or discourage
positive marriage and family patterns and values? _____

Which symbols express the relationships
that might occur between family members? _____

Advertising

Much advertising attempts to associate a particular image of family or marriage
with the need to purchase the advertiser's product or service. Often the implica-
tion is that you (and your partner) will be happy or successful only if you do
whatever the advertising suggests.

In contrast, public service advertisements usually seek to enlist a person in worthwhile efforts for community improvement or for better health. These announcements may suggest ways in which a marriage or family can be improved or more
successful.

Advertising assumptions about
marriage and family values: _____.

Influence of this advertisement
on most couples or families: _____.

EDUCATION FOR MARRIAGE AND FAMILY IN SOCIETY

As you have discovered in your journey through this workbook, your family and
community educated you for marriage long before you met your spouse. Consider
the quality of marriage and family education that is now provided in your locality.

Schools: Public and Private

Think about your formal educational experience, and then examine what schools
are now doing to help children, youths, and adults succeed in marriage and cre-

ate healthy family situations. As part of your concern about family life education in your schools, you may interview a teacher, counselor, or administrator in a public or private school.

I will focus on this school: _____.

Courses in family living, marriage, human
sexuality, communication skills, interpersonal relations: _____.

Attitudes of school about
marriage and family relationships: _____.

Informal family education conveyed by
students, teachers, and others in the school: _____.

How parents can encourage the school to
improve its marriage and family education: _____.

Churches and Synagogues

Many churches and synagogues have programs to support marriage and family living. You might interview a clergyperson or other staff person in a church or synagogue in your area. Here are some topics on which you might secure information.

My church and its programs are _____.

Examples of its success or failure
in family-related areas are _____.

How has the program changed? _____

How can I assist in these programs? _____

COMMUNITY AGENCIES AND
MARRIAGE AND FAMILY LIVING

In addition to fire, medical, court system, and basic governmental services, your community probably has several agencies and professional persons to provide services to couples, children, youths, adults, and families.

Community Agencies

Where are the marriage and family agencies in your community? If possible, talk with police, attorneys, judges, or other professional persons who are involved in the legal systems that relate to marriage and family concerns.

A community agency or person involved in family issues: _____.

How this person works with couples, families,
and/or children to improve family conditions: _____.

Ways society can improve its laws and
legal procedures relating to family matters: _____.

Important issues concerning marriage, family,
divorce, child support, and other family areas: _____.

Police Work with Families

Police officers are often called to scenes of domestic disturbances and violence between family members. Interceding between spouses in cases of domestic disturbance is the most dangerous work that police officers do because often the spouses who are fighting each other will unite in harming the intervening police officers.

You will gain a deeper appreciation of the difficulties in coping with violence if you can talk with a professional person who is with the police or probation department in your community.

Professional law enforcement person: _____.

How this person's work relates to family situations: _____.

How crime and family quality are related: _____.

Ways society can enable this person
or agency to work better with families: _____.

QUALITY OF LIFE FOR FAMILIES

There are many indicators of the quality of life for couples and families in a community. Here are some examples.

Are parks safe, clean, well-maintained, and
easily available to children and families? _____

Community events for families include _____.

Other ways my community supports
positive marriage and family living are _____.

If you care enough about solving the crises in the world, you can reach out to other families and enable them to find joy and happiness.

HOW WILL YOU REACH OUT IN YOUR COMMUNITY?

These suggestions may guide you and your spouse as you consider your next steps for reaching out in the community.

Goals I want to accomplish are _____.

The type of group in which I want to work is _____.

Similar projects I have seen or read about are _____.

Materials I need or can create for this project are _____.

Others with whom I can work for these goals are _____.

Specific plan, schedule, and outline of the project are _____.

Chapter 42

Your Longer Range Plans

"Paul, look at all the stars," Cathy exclaimed as she paused to let the waves tickle her toes. "They have been there for centuries."

"Yeah," Paul confirmed as he squeezed her hand. "It's hard to imagine what we'll be doing even ten years from now."

"Well, by then all our children will be in school, and I'll be in my career full time." Cathy added, "You'll probably be manager of a bigger office."

"Your career and the children, yes," validated Paul. "I'm not so sure about the manager idea."

The moonlight caught Cathy's slight smile as she scrutinized Paul's face. "What distant stars do I see in your eyes?"

"You are there for sure," Paul reassured, drawing her closer. "I'm wondering how we can help others have as much fun together as we do."

Through your marriage, you and your spouse support each other in the spiritual journey. As you saw in Parts 1 and 2, you shape your marital journey toward your future with decisions about yourself in relation to God, your marriage, children, and the world. These decisions are your faith foundation for your spiritual journey.

When you are open (humble, teachable, and willing), the Holy Spirit fills you with power to enact your choices. You improve your resources by increasing your positives and stopping your negatives. This is your spiritual formation.

For me, marriage and spiritual
formation are related in these ways: _____.

For my spouse, marriage and spiritual
formation are related in these ways: _____.

```
    P
 L  O  V  E
    W
    E
    R
```

*Walk in love, as Christ also has loved us
and given Himself for us (Eph. 5:2).*

Since you have journeyed through this workbook, you now know how your communication connects the four basic love power dimensions. You know how to enrich your marriage and where to go for help when you need it. You have thought about how you can extend love power to your children, to other couples, and to the world.

My love for my spouse is deepening in these ways: _____.

My spouse has matured in love in these ways: _____.

How I feel about these changes: _____.

In this chapter you and your spouse can reflect on your workbook minijourney as your discoveries and increased skills apply to your future. By having longer range goals and plans, you can prepare for the inevitable transitions, differentiations, and integrations that are a normal part of your marital journey spiraling upward to your ultimate goal of becoming perfected in love.

UPDATING YOUR TIME LINES

What will you do with your life? Begin with where you are now and add other marks on your time line to indicate significant points in your life.

Consider the next several years of your lives. At each point indicated, enter the two or three most important events that you want to happen (or perhaps that you are afraid might happen). Then discuss your entries.

The fruit of the Spirit is love, joy, peace, longsuffering, kindness, goodness, faithfulness, gentleness, self-control. . . . If we live in the Spirit, let us also walk in the Spirit. Let us not become conceited, provoking one another, envying one another (Gal. 5:22–26).

Date		Wife	Mutual	Husband
_____	Six months from now	_____	_____	_____
_____	One year from now	_____	_____	_____
_____	Two to four years from now	_____	_____	_____
_____	Five to ten years from now	_____	_____	_____
_____	Ten to twenty years from now	_____	_____	_____
_____	Other: _____	_____	_____	_____

Among possible events are career changes, promotions, education, birth of a child, death of a relative, moving, major purchases, social events, and community service activities. Which events would you *not* want? Which do you fear?

Changes we may face soon are _____.

Changes we can avoid are _____.

Ways we can plan for them are _____.

Thinking about them does not mean that events must happen exactly as planned. Many factors unknown to you now can enter your future and be the occasion for changes in your intentions, goals, and hopes.

When I think about the future, I feel _____.

Concerning the future, my spouse feels _____.

Talking about the future allows you and your spouse to compare goals and expectations about both big and small things. Clear goals that are mutually agreed enable you to plan your life journeys in directions that will be mutually supportive while minimizing conflicting expectations.

You are growing in love when you replace the question, "Do you love me?" with your clear affirmation, "I love you."

WHAT KIND OF LOVE?

Love of God, spouse, children, friends, and family members can give you a purpose, a sense of belonging, and satisfaction in life. Continuing your journey as a couple will challenge you to hang in there and not give up. Along your journey you can recognize and appreciate each other's gifts and have fun.

What kind of love do you want? What kind of love does your spouse want? Here are some possible answers to these questions. Circle the answers you like and invite your spouse to do the same. Then talk about your visions of love and marriage.

A love we want is a love that

- awakes and excites.

- blesses and values us.

- challenges us to live and lead.

- lasts in all situations.

- draws us to peak experiences.

- celebrates our uniqueness.

- remembers the good things.

- accepts us as we are.

- gives opportunities to grow.

- opens us to new ways to care.

- amazes and transforms us.

- brings pleasant surprises.

- speaks the truth in kindness.

- searches ways to show kindness.

- refuses to be discouraged.

- invites us to be open.

- values us as of immeasurable worth.

- sees new possibilities.

```
P
L  O V  E          A vision without a task is a dream. A task
W                  without a vision is drudgery. But a vision
E                  with a task is the hope of the world.
R
```

PERSONAL FAITH

Faith as trust emerges out of your previous experiences and continues to develop throughout your lifetime. Hope emerges when you have a clear vision for your future and confidence in your abilities to reach your vision.

Your beliefs are the principles you live by. You might write out your basic beliefs and then compare them to the beliefs of your spouse. Are there any creeds or wise sayings that you use to live by? Can you state briefly your creed?

My creed is _____.

I apply this in our lives together by _____.

What are your ultimate concerns?

My spouse and I participate
in our church in these ways: _____.

At home we celebrate our faith in these ways: _____.

Ways I am most aware of God's leading are _____.

I pray _____.

Share meditation and prayer time together as you celebrate your lives together and look toward your future.

PEAK EXPERIENCES

Peak experiences are personal experiences that are so compelling and important for you that you rearrange your life perspectives around them.

My most peak experience was _____.

It influences our marriage now in these ways: _____.

YOUR LONGER RANGE PLANS 273

> *Go therefore and make disciples of all the nations, . . . teaching them to observe all things that I have commanded you; and lo, I am with you always (Matt. 28:19–20).*

MARRIAGE LIFESTYLE APPRECIATIONS

Describe some of the qualities and behaviors that you most appreciate in your partner.

_____

In what ways does each partner initiate fun, excitement, and surprises in your relationship?

_____

How do you celebrate the special uniqueness of yourselves and your relationship?

_____

Describe a time when your partner especially listened to you as you expressed your concerns, pain, sadness, or worries.

_____

How do you usually resolve conflicts between you and your partner? Of what are you most aware when you and your spouse discuss difficult topics?

_____

In what ways are you and your partner most alike? most different?

_____

What makes you the most afraid or threatened in your relationship? What is the greatest danger or threat to your relationship?

_____

In five or ten years from now, what do you want your relationship to be? What do you want to be doing? What would you like to accomplish?

_____

What keeps you together? What do you consider to be the most important elements in your marriage?

_____

How are you filling the world with love power?

_____

P
L O V E   *As a couple, we pray for the grace and*
W   *guidance to grow in love and use our*
E   *power to transform adversities into*
R   *positives for the future.*

May God continue to bless you in all your life journeys.

If you would like to fill out the Christian Commitment Certificate, see pages 244 and 245.

Appendix

Love Power Multimedia Package

Pathways to Love Power gives you the advantages of interactive computer activities and games for your personal and marital growth. Based on your personalized input via computer, you and your partner can obtain more specific immediate feedback on all areas of your relationship.

Games and inventories enable you and your partner to compare your views and clarify your values.

This flexible system provides special sets of questions for couples according to whether they are dating, engaged, just married, or married for many years. Other sets of questions focus on the unique concerns of couples who have children from a previous marriage.

The *Pathways to Love Power* dialogue games can strengthen your communication skills and assist you in money management and budget planning. An annual calendar enables you to keep up with birthdays, anniversaries, plans, and celebrations. A special section provides viewer's guides for several popular marriage-related movies that you can rent.

Pathways to Love Power is available on an IBM compatible 3.5" high-density disk and in multimedia CD-ROM disk with sound.

To order Love Power resources, telephone (818) 584-5330 and ask for "Love Power." Inquiries and orders may also be addressed to the authors at:

> Division of Marriage and Family
> Fuller Seminary
> 180 N. Oakland Avenue
> Pasadena, CA 91101